UNDERSTANDING GRIEF
FROM A
CHRISTIAN PERSPECTIVE

MY HEAD KNOWS IT

BUT MY HEART CAN'T UNDERSTAND

Julie L. Bell

My Heart Know It
But My Heart Can't Understand
Understanding Grief from a Christian Perspective

Copyright © 2023 Julie L. Bell

All rights reserved. No part of this publication may be reproduced, distributed or transmitted in any form or by any means, without prior written permission.

Published by
Dreamer Reign Media, LLC
P.O. Box 291354
Port Orange, FL 32129

www.dreamerreign.com

For Worldwide Distribution
Printed in the U.S.A.

ISBN: 9781952253270
Library of Congress: 2023930882

TABLE OF CONTENTS

Dedication 5
Foreword 6
Preface 9
Thought 1: Loss is complicated 11
Thought 2: What Do I need right now? 15
Thought 3: Waking up to the reality of grief
and friends 23
Thought 4: Questions and painful memories 29
Thought 5: Jesus the Human 35
Thought 6: Funerals and closure 43
Thought 7: Grief from where I see it 49
Thought 8: When emotions die 55
Thought 9: Caretaker for the wounded soul 59
Thought 10: Let's talk about the "D" word 65
Thought 11: Nothing personal, just business 71
Thought 12: Depression and religion don't mix ... 83
Thought 13: Precious memories and amazing grace 93
Thought 14: The season for me-time 103
Thought 15: Family feud 107
Thought 16: Where do I go from here? 111
Thought 17: Help me! 115
Thought 18: The morning after 119
Thought 19: Acceptance 123
Thought 20: Auto-pilot moments 129

TABLE OF CONTENTS CONT.

Thought 21: Loss is bigger than death 133
Thought 22: Healing for the grief that suddenly found me 139
Thought 23: The costume of strength 145
Thought 24: Battered, bruised, blessed 151
Thought 25: Finally 155
Conclusion 163

DEDICATION

"Thank you" to my best friend, (Benjamin Cecil Bell Jr.) that has been walking me through my grief. During the early days of my loss, he checked on me all day, brought me food, and was so understandingly patient. I am most grateful for my spouse who knows how to pray for his wife when there are no words he could say to make me feel better. He is truly the love of my life. This is just another chapter in our story of life. Thank you "Sweet" for everything. I love you forever; this book is dedicated to you. After 40 years of marriage, you never cease to amaze me with your love and support.

Thank you to everyone that brought food, tables, chairs, and took me out for a while. You offered all of the prayers and acts of kindness during the passing of my dad. You have no idea how valuable it has been to my heart. To all my sisters that were holding my head above water and helping me make it day to day, you know who you are...I love you to life. You did something amazing for me in a time when I was totally lost and vulnerable. You protected me from myself when I needed you the most.

FOREWORD

My upbringing is that of strong spiritual influence. My parents raised me to be a Christian, Pentecostal, no doubt. The people I spent most of my time around represented three to five generations of spiritual people. Many of my teachers did not die until I was twenty. They lived well into their eighties and nineties. I attended many of their services as this was part of the culture. I was not aware that my lens was colored when it comes to death and dying. I was there to hear people refer to death as the body sleeping and the spirit living on in the great "by and by."

For the good part of three decades, I beheld as people paraded in front of the casket during Homegoing celebrations. Many crying, some even dancing, others crumbling to the floor. All this while people declared, "to be absent from the body is to be present with the Lord." Ministers would say things like, "God picked a flower from His garden for Himself." I would hear people demand that their families be strong and "there will be no crying and falling out today."

I am amazed at the pointed understanding and relevance I find in this book, "My Head knows it, but my Heart Can't Understand." This is such a refreshing and realistic look at the effect of death on those who remain. As I reached adulthood, and declared my faith in Jesus Christ, the sayings and the varied responses to loss of life became quite the conundrum for me. As I entered into the ministry, death and the existential nature of Christian philosophy — combined with my limited understanding of its implications became quite evident. As I ministered to people, I parroted what I heard my predecessors say. I was ill-prepared to assist people outside of my faith tradition with the grieving process. 15 years in, I finally took a class in death and dying taught by some brilliant people who did not originate in my spiritual camp. They caused me to laugh, cry, and to reflect; they moved me forward. They caused me to take a critical look at my understanding of death.

Death is not evil. It is a reality we would do well to address. I now know that the experiences are varied, both personal and subjective. I learned so much. I am now a professional practitioner in the helping of others.

This tool that you are about to access, will refresh you. It will restore your faith in the ability to live with pain; you can manage and use it to bless others. This project is about personal quest for freedom, faith, and forging ahead. I wish I had access to this book in 1995; it would have changed my life. Julie, the author, is one of those rare persons who is willing to say, "The Emperor has no clothes on." She refuses to provide fluff. She has suffered, survived, and is regaining her strength. Julie Bell has decided to produce fullness.

Theology is not enough if it is not addressing reality. This book is purposeful and practical. It will peel away the layers of pain and place you on a higher plane.

It will reveal, restore, and revive. This book will give you access to liberty you never dreamed you could have.

Reverend Dr. Benjamin C. Bell Jr.
Co-founder of Dads With A Purpose

PREFACE

In this book, each chapter begins with a thought. It will help you focus in on what I have to say. Take time to really think about the sections, as each one is designed to address different aspects of this transition called grief.

This book was not written to be read in any specific order. Some sections you may not be able to deal with right now, or maybe it doesn't apply to your specific situation. Go ahead and skip that section and come back to it at another time. Other information I've shared, you may certainly need it later when dealing with someone else.

Grief does not just happen when someone dies, but whenever we lose something meaningful to us. The loss may be a job, home, business, or anything that made us feel secure, accomplished, or loved.

I understand it may be difficult to truly comprehend or process grief in the early stages. It's okay to cry, to feel, to experience things that you weren't ready or able to walk through before. It is all part of the healing journey after a loss. Open yourself up, and give your heart permission to be human.

Pain is not pleasant, but ignoring it doesn't make it go away. It will wait patiently to be heard, understood, then released. I hope this book helps you or someone you love. Writing it helped me; it actually saved me. My prayer is that you can begin to heal.

THOUGHT 1
Loss is complicated

I thought I knew, but I found out what I "know," is not <u>all</u> there is to know.

Life is an interesting series of unforeseen turns. Most of the time, the path we end up on we would have never selected if given the option. There is really no way to know what will happen during the courses of our lives. Some things feel unbearable in the moment we experience them.

Our minds struggle to make sense out of it just so we can handle the unbelievable pressure. Our heart screams out and our brain struggles to decode the purpose of such pain; taking the next breath can be exasperating. We discover the same experience with death in the lives of others, how it affects each of them in a different way. How can that be? We process these events differently according to what works for us. Maybe it doesn't work—we are just trying to get through it, moment by moment.

There are no written rules of order for the grief process. Reactions differ as wide as the spectrum of different colors. All of them are a part of the landscape of grieving.

As we begin to navigate our way through our personal journeys, we find significant differences and glaring similarities. What happened to me may not have happened to you, and vice versa. We all had an upbringing. For some, it was nurturing and loving. For others, it was traumatic and difficult. Our authority figures molded our thought process to judge what was right and wrong—what was logical, and what was nonsense.

> *"Learning to cope with our triumphs and tragedies is the normal course of our lives."*

Some people have experienced unimaginable trauma early on in life. Their brain handles life's pressure in an entirely different way. Our early days shaped our brain system to process things through the lens of our memory. Studies have shown that it is not only our thought memory, but there is a chemical memory that takes place in the brain during stressful situations. During the moments of stress, the brain is "programmed" how to respond whenever we experience trigger pressures that remind us of childhood experiences. The same chemicals are released during these stress peaks and bathe the

THOUGHT 1: LOSS IS COMPLICATED

brain; our brain then goes into a responsive protective mode. Instinctively, we begin to process the situation in a manner that is familiar to us. We may have determined what is the right way or wrong way to do things according to what was modeled in front of us. We may have made decisions early in life that were comfortable for our personality or belief system based on experience. In times of crisis, we tend to fall back on our history to help us make a reasonable decision with what we are now experiencing. We determine what our standards are, and what our moral compass says. Most of the time, we don't know any other way to be.

> *"Most of the time, we don't know any other way to be."*

Learning to cope with our triumphs and tragedies is the normal course of our lives. As we live, these occurrences cannot be avoided. Sooner or later, they show up; we must begin to process these things internally. Everything in between these events can be fairly smooth. However, it may seem as if tragedy is a constant or all too frequent visitor. Truthfully, it can be just one long season of sequential losses that weigh heavily on our hearts.

We have hardly had time to grieve over the last incident while the next one is knocking on our heart's door! The constant, agonizing feeling of loss can cause us to believe that we are always on the losing end of things, while others around us, appear to be thriving. Our hearts can be seemingly drained of all emotion except grief and lingering sadness. The brain interprets losses as constant, even though time has passed between the incidents. These are the loud, internal, silent voices of our emotions that direct our paths into uncharted territory. Our head is trying to speak logic to our reasoning brain, but our emotional heart won't stop hurting.

"The first step to becoming wise is to look for wisdom, so use everything you have to get understanding." Proverbs 4:7 ERV

 **PRAYER**

Dear God,

I'm asking You for clarity in a lot of areas. These steps to recover from my grief may be new to me, but I recognize I have to start somewhere. I am learning more each day about myself and others. Please help me not to pull away from this process but direct me as I am opening my heart and my mind to what I need to learn. I do know that I hurt on the inside from my loss; I need help with this. My thoughts are all over the place, and none of this makes sense right now. Please help me to walk one day at a time through this fog of confusion. Thank You in advance for listening. Amen.

THOUGHT 2
What do I need right now?

If you asked me if I needed anything...I do, prayer. My heart is hurting today. Thanks.

Everyone asks, "What do you need?" It is usually the closing statement of most conversations with a grieving person. This is what we have been taught to ask. Individual needs, as far as support from others, can be a mystery. How can one possibly know what to ask for at a moment like this? External support is critical. We need to understand that people may need to come to us later after they have had the opportunity to clearly evaluate our needs. Keep in mind, it is not easy to ask for help. *Futuristically, when you make an offer of help, be sure that you are willing to follow through with your words.*

When people come to our aid after a recent loss, all advice may sound like muffled words blowing in the wind. We may not be sure how to act or react. Our emotions are unpredictable and inconsistent. People start flooding into our once personal and private space, even though they have not been invited. We may scramble for support and compassion. While at the same time, our heart is wide open to injury; others should tread lightly. The grievous wounds that happen during this time are lasting ones that stand out in our memory. We tend to never forget what people did or didn't do, or how they made us feel.

> *"When people come to our aid after a recent loss, all advice may sound like muffled words blowing in the wind."*

I remember: just the thought of people coming into my home created a sense of panic. I started looking around as if I was planning to host a party. I began cleaning and putting things away, afraid of the condemning judgement of others about my living space. To me, the worst possible thing is having a parade of unannounced, drop-in visitors for days on end, while trying to maintain a magazine-ready home! The internal, emotional pressure was already unbearable. When I added the external pressure of well-meaning visitors to the mix, I almost totally melted down.

When we make our visits, remember this is not the time to testify about our personal loss and how badly we suffered. It is not the time to monopolize the support intended for a wounded mourner, making ourselves the center of attention. Our job is not to be a "wonderful counselor," but a concerned, comforting friend. The statement of "I know how you feel" almost turns the tables to make the person pressing through a fresh loss, search for words of comfort for the person making the statement. The truth is, at that moment, nobody really cares about our history of loss because they are dealing with their own tragedies. To them, every moment feels eternal. They just want to wake up from this nightmare hoping that none of it is real; but it is.

Nights bleed into days on end, with no sleep in between. Mourners long to remember the way their loved one's voice sounded and the last thing they said to them. They squeeze their eyes tightly shut just to picture their face as their words gradually begin to fade into the foggy shadows. Clothing and familiar smells are points of soothing, especially in the early days. There is no written rule book for the sufferer, or the friend on exactly how to handle the bruised heart; just be careful. Although the mourner's heart is still beating, every painful rhythm is a reminder that they are still here, and their loved one has gone.

I have witnessed tremendous pain and disbelief written all over their faces. I have heard the curdling screams reverberate into the cold, night air as they tried to release the pressure of fresh grief. This is the time to reassure them that we are with them for the long term, good or bad. Try not to show panic as the grief-stricken is walking through the ugly place of death; it is final and permanent. This reality may take a while to set in. The griever may continue to function, completing necessary tasks, and making critical decisions. *People can continue to function, almost robotically.* As they become more aware of the void, internal pain then resurrects. Most likely, the mourner is discovering the new silence that is left behind along with a shattered heart. Again, external support is critical during these days. Learn how to be present and supportive in their moments of awakening.

Grieving people often don't know what they need at that moment, or what they will need later. Don't judge them for their weak moments or reactions that you may not understand. What is always needed is prayer and considerate support.

One of the worst experiences is the death of someone close to us. This can occur at any time during your life. I don't know why it is so difficult to accept death as something that's normal. It's not like we can live forever. We begin dying the moment we are born. As an adult, we feel as if we should be able to handle this because it is part of the life cycle. We are born. We live—we die. This seems logical, right? We may have read about death in books, even in the Bible. We may think we are prepared having lost someone more distant and been through the "process" of death and funerals. Funerals tend to compartmentalize our emotions into one event then everyone just moves on. However, the passing of someone really close to our heart leaves so many lingering questions, thoughts, and unexplainable feelings about death. The deep pain and anguish we feel is often unexpected and surprising. It can be a total shock to our system, mental, emotional and physical. We may begin to wonder if the weight of losing someone dear to us will ever leave us or get better. The death whether sudden or expected from a long-term illness, seems to leave a noticeable void in our lives that can't be filled. The pressure of the loss is a constant companion both unwanted and wanted. Unwanted, because it simply hurts so bad knowing this person is gone permanently. Wanted, because we are afraid that the absence of pain may signal we have forgotten about the person while attempting to move on with our modified life. The pain we experience is different than anything we have really felt before. It is a deep groaning of our soul. We struggle to pen the words that can accurately describe the ghostly presence of this dark emotional place. The feeling of loss never seems to totally leave us. It just fades into the background more and more until we can handle the thought of it in our daily life.

> *"Most likely, the mourner is discovering the new silence that is left behind along with a shattered heart."*

When we are usually the strong one in a group of our peers, they may struggle with hearing that we are not doing well. We can sense their feeling of panic when they must find words of comfort that have meaning for either of us. The words are often full of comfortable, old quotes we've heard others say to someone that is grieving. It is difficult, especially if they have no personal experience, and even if they do, each person processes grief in a different way. Too often we find ourselves saying, "I know how you feel." This is never a true statement though it is well intended. I cringe whenever I hear this statement because it feels so selfish. It is not their pain, it is yours!

The most critical stage is the early moments of someone's loss. I call this the Intensive Care Stage. Their heart is throbbing in pain that they could never have imagined existed and their ears are growing foggy. It is tough for them to remember the last sentence someone just said because nothing makes sense.

"Blessed are they that mourn: for they shall be comforted."
Matthew 5:4 KJV

# PRAYER

Dear God,

In the early days of my loss, I confess I am lost. My emotions are all over the place and I can't really explain the hole I feel in my heart. People have no idea what this feels like to me. If I'm going to be honest with You, I'm struggling to just keep going every day. I hurt so terribly bad in my heart I can hardly stand it. I just need You to hold me up right now because I'm falling apart. I never really knew death could take so much from me all at once. When is this feeling going to stop? I hate this! As I search for understanding, help me to be patient with myself. Grieving takes time and healing must be a process because I don't see anything good happening right now. I am overwhelmed by the circumstances that surround me. Be my comfort when no one else understands my emptiness and incredible sadness. The weight of this is too much for me to carry alone. Guide me through this dark place of sadness. Amen.

MY HEAD KNOWS IT

THOUGHT 3
WAKING UP TO THE REALITY OF GRIEF AND FRIENDS

I wish I could wake up and none of this was happening right now. At least I have my friends, right?

It is an unfortunate truth that emotional trauma is difficult for people to deal with, especially when it happens to a close friend. Things that happen in the mind are not as obvious as a physical illness. We may discover that it is easier to have superficial conversations rather than listen to the words of deep anguish that we don't have an answer for. Our minds may scramble for meaningful, appropriate words and phrases that will somehow ease the suffering of our friend. Some things in our history of friendship have been "easy fixes." However, we are terribly unprepared for the bigger emotional responsibility of comforting a grieving friend.

We may find ourselves overshadowed with a sense of incompetence in our friend's time of greatest need.

When grief arrives in the relationship, we might find ourselves attempting to just end the conversation because we are literally squirming in discomfort. Next to the pain happening to us, the worst thing is watching a dear friend or family member battling with the despair of deep loss. The feelings of anguish and helplessness are unwanted visitors in a close friendship. They don't show up often but when they do, they knock us off our square of balance. Our minds often carry us back to pleasurable memories of wonderful experiences together that brought us close to each other. These are only temporary reprises from the current tragic situation. We think good times are the definition of a solid relationship. In fact, the negative experiences galvanize the authentic value that is found only in relationships that have passed through the fires of life and survived. The bond of love with a friend often exceeds the connection we experience with our blood family. The rough times that challenge our relationships should cause them to rise to the top, even when we don't know exactly what to do or say. Realize it is okay not to have all the answers; we should make our ears available and our hearts open to grieve their loss with them.

> *"The rough times that challenge our friendship should cause our relationship to rise to the top even when we don't know exactly what to do or say."*

THOUGHT 3: WAKING UP THE REALITY OF GRIEF AND FRIENDS

In my own recent experience with grief and loss, I found that people I thought were reasonably close to me really did not know what to say. I saw the panic in their eyes as they realized I was having frail moments. These weren't just mild episodes. I'm talking about full-blown, spontaneous melt downs! It was just as uncomfortable for me to experience them, as it was for others to watch. I wish I could've controlled them, but those low moments blind-sided me from out of nowhere! My friends tried to comfort me but their simple physical touch collapsed my already fragile emotions.

Usually I am strong, confident, organized, and encouraging to others. Ministry is what I was born to do, and I love it. Throughout the years, there was always time for good conversation, good food, and inspiration from God. However, my personal loss shook me to my core. I couldn't access any of the qualities that I was accustomed to accessing. I scrambled to grasp the concepts of hope that I used numerous times to help other people. A new place of fragmented thoughts and feelings took over my once solid mental abilities. My emotional footing was slipping into a deep pit. I felt my soul unraveling like a pulled string in a crochet scarf. I was helpless to stop it, even though I knew it was happening. I had not been prepared for this moment in my life. This place was new; it was unfamiliar to me. I had been around so many others as they walked through

> *"I scrambled to grasp the concepts of hope that I used so many times to help other people."*

their grief, but it had never come this close to me before. I found out grief was real and had an identity of its own.

I had seen the shockingly blank stare of "this can't be real" as the widower numbly walked toward the casket one last time. I had watched the toll of loss begin to suck the life force out of the one left behind, because their memories were all that was left to hold on to.

This time, it was my nightmare. I wanted to wake up and go back to my life as it used to be before death. I needed (somehow) to find my way through this reality of deep pain. It was not a dream; it was very real. Worst of all, I was not ready for any of the emotions that took over my life! I was on the edge of insanity. My mind screamed, "Somebody please walk with me through this and listen, listen, listen." I needed someone to hear my heart and share my tears. I didn't know how to ask for help.
My grief had a voice that needed to be heard, without judgement. I wanted to scream, but my pain couldn't find its voice. I realized if I was going to survive this experience, I couldn't place the responsibility solely on my friends. I had to search out the answer for myself. I had no idea where to begin. I just knew I wanted to survive this experience. I had never felt so lost in my entire life.

A true friend is always loyal, and a brother is born to help in time of need. Proverbs 17:17 TLB

THOUGHT 3: WAKING UP THE REALITY OF GRIEF AND FRIENDS

 **PRAYER**

Dear God,

Someone told me, You are an amazing friend. I want to know You as that. I have a lot of questions. My loss has left me wondering if I will ever be okay again. Before this happened, I guess I have never really talked to You this deep before, but I am in a place of darkness that I need to recover from. What people see on the outside is not what I feel on the inside. I am smiling but I am not alright. I know my friends are trying their best, but it's not enough. I am alone in a room full of people. I give You permission to be the type of friend I can tell anything to. I feel You listening, even now. My thoughts are all over the place. I'm trying hard to find relief from this pressure that is driving me insane. It's eating me up a little more every day that goes by. I thought I had it all together, but I feel like I was just faking it sometimes. I need to be whole again, but right now I cry a lot. I'm simply exhausted. Is that normal? I know my tears don't make You nervous, so I am learning to open up to You. I'm glad this is just between us right now because I can't explain this to anybody else. Thanks for listening. We'll talk again soon. Amen.

MY HEAD KNOWS IT

THOUGHT 4
Questions and painful memories

I know they are in a better place, but those of us who are left are struggling with their precious memories.

"It's never easy when it's your turn. My father passed away peacefully yesterday afternoon. Sleep well to the legend I simply knew as "daddy." He made our lives magical with his inventions, construction projects, magic tricks and hugs. He taught me everything I know about music and the church, loving God, His Word, and loving your family...and fixing stuff! I have a hot pink toolbox now because of him. I started playing the organ for church at the age of thirteen, just so I could take the pressure off my daddy while he preached. He didn't have a musician behind him, so I promised him if he would buy a Hammond Organ for the church, I would commit to learning how to play it for church. It changed my life! I will always carry his words and his clarion preaching voice in my heart. He wasn't called the "Flying Preacher" for nothing! He was an amazing gospel preacher. I know his reward is great, and his crown of righteousness looks incredible on him. Momma, we're going to be alright, we got you. "Pray for us as we struggle to go on without him. 'We don't sorrow as others that have no hope,' but we do grieve. Even Jesus wept. We are a strong family, full of pastors and leaders, but please allow us to be human during this time. This time, we need you to pray for us."

Those were my words in a very candid moment right after my dad died. When I look back at them, I realize that even in that space I had a guarded answer. I guess that's what I knew to do in that moment. Every one of us will have our turn with death.

When someone close dies it really shakes you. People always say to "remember the good times." They mean well. Really, they do. Isn't that what we are supposed to say in times like this? Maybe I should restate that. Isn't that what we have been taught to say? We have heard it said hundreds of times.

Our memories can be wonderful, yet haunting. I cannot tell you how many days I longed to go back to that simple time as I remember it, so carefree and happy. Again, loss is real and so are the memories. They can be hard to stomach and evoke emotions of joy, but also much sadness and anger. "Why did God take them? I

THOUGHT 4: QUESTIONS AND PAINFUL MEMORIES

mean really, I know some really horrible people that have lived longer!" Some questions have no answers.

Our memories can be the hardest to process; they never go away. Many, many times, I have avoided even driving down the street where I grew up because I couldn't tolerate the emotions when I looked at my childhood home. I remembered riding my bike up and down the sidewalk, dinners on the patio, the sound of my dad's power saw in the garage as he worked on yet another construction project, the smell of the cedar walls in his basement prayer room, the magic tricks with quarters he would pull from behind our ears, running to the door when he drove up in the next new station wagon (lol), the grace he prayed as we sat around the dining room table, the blue glass pieces he bought my mom every wedding anniversary. There is a picture of my dad and mother smiling posted on the wall in his church. They meant well, honoring the person that pastored the church. Sometimes, I had to quickly turn away, so I didn't see it because it hurt badly. I felt the tears well up in my soul. It was all just too much for my heart. I never knew happy thoughts could torment you, until now.

Family is extremely important; it is the foundation for building a wonderful life. Passing on rich traditions and values is critical to building a strong future for the next generation. When you lose an important piece of the family puzzle, you know your picture is now incomplete. When you look at the picture, you don't focus on what is there, only the piece that is missing. The actual piece must now be replaced by the memory of what it felt and looked like.

You may struggle to comprehend what your future will be like without that critical piece. The process your brain goes through attempting to come to the point of acceptance of the loss, takes more time than we like to allow. Joy will return, just not immediately. Shattered hearts need support and loving care to mend. The scar may remain, but healing is a constant friend. One day memories won't hurt so much.

> *"Shattered hearts need support and loving care to mend."*

It is hard when you come to the reality that a page in your life has turned. If we had known that they would be gone from our life, we would have done so many things differently. It's really God's goodness that doesn't allow us to know when someone will be taken from us. That is too big of a burden for anyone to carry. There are so many unanswered questions that we may never know the answers to. Don't get frustrated. Most people don't get an answer. I guess it just feels better to ask them anyway, just to get it off our chest. My head knows this, but my heart is not ready to understand. It's too soon right now.

Precious in the sight of the LORD is the death of his saints.
Psalms 116:15 KJV

THOUGHT 4: QUESTIONS AND PAINFUL MEMORIES

 **PRAYER**

Dear God,

Today is not a good day. If I'm going to be truthful with You, I'm angry. This whole process has taken such a toll on me. How could You take them? It's not fair! Others have lived longer, and they're not even good people. It hurts so bad and I'm really trying to understand your wisdom in all of this. My good memories of times gone by are just too much for my heart to process. Some days, it takes all of my strength just to take another breath and live with this incredible sorrow! I'm struggling today and I'm crying out to the same God I'm mad at! It doesn't make sense. I feel like I'm faking this relationship with You because I'm struggling with my faith. I guess this is all part of my healing. I didn't know opening up would hurt so badly. God, I'm really trying. I really don't know what to do with all this pain that is coming to the surface; it makes me sick. I really need help. Amen.

MY HEAD KNOWS IT

THOUGHT 5
Jesus the human

The biggest discovery is the pain and loss we feel when someone close to us dies. The truth is, you never know how you will react until it happens. We have been conditioned to be strong. Truthfully, do we shut down expressing our sorrow because it makes others uncomfortable?

Recently I had a couple of friends lose a child suddenly and unexpectedly. My recent losses were slow and agonizing. The common thread in both situations is really the human experience. Some of us have been formally trained how to deal with grief. We really believe in our hearts that because of our formal training, we are better equipped to deal with it on a personal level when it occurs.

However, one thing I have discovered is the personal shock and confusion that arrives in every person when they try to cope with an extremely personal loss. No one prepares us for the reality of the new levels of pain and despair we feel. Our mind swirls with the "what if's" and "if I'd only's" that are stuck on repeat in our heads. No one tells us that tomorrow hurts just as bad as yesterday. No one warned us of the sudden outbursts of heartbreak that happen when we see their picture, or when someone asks us how they are doing because they didn't know they passed away. Nobody told us how hard it would be to get out of bed every day and try not to dwell in the place of sorrow. No one prepared us for the brutally honest human experience of living with a hole in our souls.

When my father died, the Bible seemed different to me. I began to understand what it meant by saying, "For we do not have a High Priest who cannot sympathize with our weaknesses, but was in all points tempted as we are, yet without sin." Hebrews 4:15 (NKJV). Jesus is our High Priest that was sent to earth just for us. There were so many things He needed to accomplish during his time on earth, both naturally and spiritually. He gave us a blueprint for successful living in this earth. There are times we must remember we are all human and we must take time away for ourselves. Our weakness can show up when we don't expect it. Those are the times we must reflect and take the time to heal because something inside

THOUGHT 5: JESUS THE HUMAN

needs our attention.

When it comes to Jesus, we can be so caught up in His deity of being God's Son, that we miss His humanity. No matter how great you are to everyone else, it is important to remember you are human. Jesus had many emotional experiences while He was on the earth, just like us. He understood betrayal, gossip, and even being used by people who didn't really like Him. They just wanted stuff from Him. He was even able to connect to the feeling of grief and loss at Lazarus' tomb. If you read the account found in John chapter 11, the loving relationship between Jesus, Mary, Martha, and Lazarus is mentioned.

I often wondered why Jesus delayed His journey to Lazarus when He heard he was terribly ill. It was always taught that Jesus did not go immediately so God would get the glory out of the miracle of the resurrection of Lazarus from the dead. This is true, but I now see another great necessity for the delay. In doing so, it ensured Jesus would experience something new to Himself, yet common to each one of us, the weight and sorrow of personal loss.

Before this incident, Jesus had not lost a loved one to death. It is different when you are an observer of grief rather than a partaker of its bitter fruit. For Jesus to have a realistic life journey reflective of ours, it had to include the sting of death. Jesus felt the brunt of the human experience as He met with Mary, arriving long after Lazarus had passed away. Imagine the words that rang in his head, "If you had been here, our brother

Lazarus wouldn't have died!" What a cutting statement coming from someone He loved so much. She was hurting so much; the words just came out! Realize, Jesus was hurting too. Words coming from people in our inner circle can cause deep pain in moments when we are vulnerable to spiritual injury. If we don't know how to process these moments coming from people who are also hurting, they can become mortal wounds. Think about the Christ discovering the manifestation of physical pain and mental anguish as He stood there. This flood of emotions resulted in an intense outburst of crying and open grieving that was observed by all in attendance that day. In that moment, Jesus became a grieving friend. Jesus wept so much, the Jews that stood around commented, "Look how He loved him" John 11:36. This was a Jesus they did not recognize. Their amazing leader now displayed His grief openly, without regret. This demonstration served an amazing purpose. It did not take away from Him being Jesus the Christ. On the contrary, it added to His resume solidifying the title as our High Priest who has been touched by emotions just like us in a similar situation.

> *"Grief can manifest in ways you never thought about before."*

Connecting with our emotions is a vital part of life. It doesn't make you weak, less spiritual or less useful, especially if you are in a leadership position; it makes you human. The release and expression of grief is an important part of healing from the death experience. Our hearts and minds need a healthy release from the pressure we experience from moment to moment. My head was beginning to know it, but my heart still struggled to understand this.

Loss like this brings life into focus. I am learning more about myself both the good and the bad. How do I fix what is truly dysfunctional in me? This is not intellect. It is emotion. All the logical things I knew, did not bring any clarity or peace in my troubled heart. Grief can manifest in ways you never thought about before:

» You may avoid social settings all together.

» You may eat too much, or not at all.

» You may sleep too much, or not at all.

» You may have physical pains and disease manifestations from internalizing all the pressure.

» You may seek out relief from the pain with medication or drugs (legal and illegal) to forget for a little while. You just want the pain to stop!

» You may become deeply spiritual or attempt to appear unphased by your trauma.

» You may engross yourself in acts of service to others or become a hermit and hide out from the world all together.

» You may walk away from your faith altogether in a cloud of confusion and internal struggle.

All of these are normal responses to the revelation that nothing you do will bring them back. They are forever gone from here. The knowledge of that simple fact, can drive you insane if you allow it to.

Our greatest struggle is the acceptance of this reality, and eventually making peace with it. We know, someday we too will die. Those we leave behind will struggle like we are right now. This is the vicious circle of life we all will face, sooner or later. My head knows it, but my heart still can't understand why.

And straightway the father of the child cried out, and said with tears, Lord, I believe; help thou mine unbelief. Mark 9:24

PRAYER

Dear God,

Today I'm trying to face myself. I see now that I am human. As I look at Jesus, He had His human moments too. I guess it is okay to cry and feel the pain of loss when someone dies. I'm not crazy. It hurts like nothing I've ever known before. I'm beginning to understand the kind of strength You've put inside. People always say to "be strong," but I'm starting to see that doesn't mean hold all of this grief inside. Being strong is learning to open up to You and let You inside. I didn't want to ever feel death like this, but it is all part of the cycle of life. I'm beginning to understand that I should trust You with my deepest pain because You know exactly what it is. I want to release this hurt that's in my gut, but I am still learning how. I feel the pressure every day, but I don't want to. Please help me to dig deeper and give all of it to You when I'm ready. Amen.

MY HEAD KNOWS IT

THOUGHT 6
Funerals and closures

There's something about getting the body in the ground that relieves some of the pressure and starts the healing process. It makes it final. I don't understand the process, but I know how I feel.

The days leading up to my father's funeral were brutal. I couldn't function and tried to keep busy so I wouldn't have to think about my daddy being gone. Emotionally, I was a wreck. People tend to hug you a lot when they come by your home to visit. They don't mean any harm, it's just what we've been taught to do. I discovered it was something I could not tolerate. The expressions of touch would bring waves of grief that were agonizing. I couldn't breathe and I felt a great sense of panic and anxiety. I found myself consistently retreating from physical contact just to maintain my composure to some degree. I don't know why it happened; it just did. A plethora of things show up that you can't quite explain while you are grieving. Even my grown children didn't know this fragile mother. I had always been such a lover of social settings. I loved cooking large meals and greeting visitors in my home. There was nothing like a great party, with lots of people eating and enjoying each other's company. Now I panicked at the sound of the doorbell, worried if my house was clean enough for the parade of well-wishers. The hidden truth is, I was worried about more melt downs and entertaining guests when my heart and body were simply exhausted. The emotional toll of putting on your game-face can push you to a mental brink of collapse. My brain was a pot of irrational thoughts that didn't connect to any central theme, all caused by my incredible grief.

    My friends didn't know this new me either. They brought over food and chairs. They helped me clean my house and prepare for the influx of people. I saw the multiple acts of service because they were at a loss for words too. Pain looks different on every person. Overall, it was a traumatic for us all.

    Funerals are strange necessities for the surviving. They bring families and friends together to honor the life of the deceased, and offer community support to the family. Every culture has its own traditions when it comes to these End Of Life Celebrations. Some are very reserved and quiet, full of rituals and soft words. Others, like what is common in black churches, are jubilant and loud. It

THOUGHT 6: FUNERALS AND CLOSURE

helps our expressive culture to release some of the pain while praising God for bringing us through the entire experience. God is strength to us during this challenging time.

The commonality of it all, is that funerals afford people the opportunity to say goodbye. Whether they take place at a church, funeral home, oceanside or graveside, these services give our hearts a chance to begin the process of releasing the body back to the Creator. We make such a grand celebration when a life enters this world; it is only fitting that there is a recognition when a life leaves this world. As difficult as the funeral process is, I don't know if I could have handled not having one. The emotional support alone helped me walk through the challenging days that were yet to occur. There is an unexplainable relief when these celebrations are over. It brings a closure of sorts which signals a start to internal healing. Though life is different from that point, it does continue. A small weight lifts as we turn a page in our history.

> *"God is strength to us during this challenging time."*

In the early months of the year 2020, a world-wide pandemic had interrupted that process. COVID-19, a highly contagious disease, caused public funerals to be banned. Now they are distant, attendance-restricted, and some are even viewed only online. I'm not sure that the lack of human physical connection and fellowship during the tradition of funerals doesn't have lasting negative

> "A plethora of things show up that you can't quite explain while you are grieving."

effects. This has taken a yet unrealized toll on the grieving process, leaving some bitter or unable to receive any closure. Others may see it as a lack of proper acknowledgement of a person's incredible life.

The practice of this "new normal" approach of dealing with death has not yet been fully felt. I believe emotional support and counseling will be needed for many months and years to come. Funerals have been a staple of death for centuries—and with good reason. During Jesus' relatively brief time on earth, it is documented that He attended several. It is part of the human expression to release the friend or family member back to the Creator. Funerals signify the attempt of the living to honor the deceased and represent the first public step of moving on after the loss. We must not forget, there is life after the funeral. Don't leave the grieving person without the support of friends and family. What you do during the weeks and months to come will make a lasting impact on how well they recover.

> "My brain was a pot of irrational thoughts that didn't connect to any central theme, all caused by my incredible grief."

THOUGHT 6: FUNERALS AND CLOSURE

Then the dust [out of which God made man's body] will return to the earth as it was, and the spirit will return to God who gave it.
Ecclesiastes 12:7 AMP

Dear God,

As I face the final moment of "good-bye" I need Your strength more than ever. A piece of me feels like it is going in the ground with them, yet another piece of me feels like I can finally take a breath. This is the hardest thing I've ever had to do. As the body begins to turn to dust my days of emptiness are just beginning. Help me cope with the aftermath of my loss after the parade of people have gone back to their lives. I am left alone with my memories and empty rooms. The funeral is just the beginning of releasing them from me. Now I must release them from my heart just enough for me to live. The tears won't seem to stop flowing so just keep me close to You right now. Those tears are helping me heal. Amen.

MY HEAD KNOWS IT

THOUGHT 7
Greif from where I see it

There is so much going on in my life right now my heart has real tears. Only the Holy Spirit gives comfort in some situations. Help me God.

As I reflect, there were some words that came from people that were of no help. I heard a lot of famous religious quotes: "God loved him best," "he's in a better place," "remember the good times," "it's going to be okay," and "we don't sorrow as others that have no hope!" What!? At this moment, when my emotions are so raw, I just need for you to be there. You don't have to say anything deep or thought provoking, just be there. You know how you imagine saying all of those things that are running through your mind, but in reality, you are just looking at them and nicely smiling? In the middle of my mental rant, I started thinking back. "Are these the things I have said so casually to people that are suffering unimaginable loss? How many times have I made some of the same statements and patted them lightly on the back?" I was horrified! I was protecting myself from connecting to their feelings of pain. Yes, I gave them a rehearsed response; it comes from conditioning. I saw this modeled by leaders in front of me, so I naturally did the same things. Afterall, that's being professional. Wait, like the professional mourners in the Bible? They showed up at funerals to cry and make a big show, but really, they weren't connected at heart. God forgive me! Now, I understand something I never saw before. I can now identify with grief from a new vantage point. A vantage point is the position where you can get a good look at something. Where you stand has everything to do with how you see something!

There really is nothing you can say to change the level of loss someone has just experienced. They have a whole life and history with the deceased that you don't know anything about. They know stories of laughter, sorrow, triumphs—losses, curious habits and talents that we never heard of or saw. Our experience with them is just a page or small chapter of their lives.

I was attending funerals quite often, but was not connecting to the experience. People's lives were more important than what I gave them credit for. Someone important to somebody had died. They were important because their life really mattered. Now, those left behind will no longer have their physical presence in their lives forever.

THOUGHT 7: GRIEF FROM WHERE I SEE IT

Frequently, I was hired to play the organ for funeral services because I was a skilled musician with lots of experience. This added pressure for me not to show emotion. I thought if I broke down emotionally, it would affect the family. I didn't want to leave them with a bad memory from the funeral of the organist falling apart, so I held it in. I believed suppressing the waves of internal sorrow was the right thing to do not realizing it was damaging my ability to truly connect to people. As I capped my expression of empathy, something strange happened. Slowly, my heart moved further away from feeling anything. My face became stoic, unmoved by the wails and outbursts of grief from the family or friends. My emotions had fallen into a comatose state, that I was powerless to awaken from.

It wasn't long before I became a professional funeral organist, playing through services with ease and collecting the check for my services at the end. I started to question who I really was, and what my motivation was for doing this. Was I so cold now that a funeral was just a payment? I thought I could just turn my feelings back on, but something inside wouldn't allow it.

I have seen the shockingly blank stare of "this can't be real" as the widow numbly walks toward the casket one last time. I have watched the toll of loss begin to suck the life force out of the one left behind, because their memories are all that is left to hold on to. Their bodies look hollow as I realize a piece of them died too that day. I realized I could watch all of this play out in front of me and not feel anything at all. My emotions had died. I'm learning to pray for them from a new perspective.

"God, give them the will to live and the strength to survive the process." We must walk with them through this and listen, listen, listen. They need someone to hear their heart and share their tears.

> *"We must walk with them through this and listen, listen, listen. They need someone to hear their heart and share their tears."*

I understand the reality of loss and compassion. It is necessary to identify with the pain of others even when it makes you uncomfortable. Their tears are real and come from a deep place that we cannot ever fully understand. It is their grief, but we can help them navigate through their unwelcome journey. We will become the support system that holds them up when they do not have their own strength to stand.

After the mourners have returned to their own lives, the real work begins. The empty home testifies of the person that lived there. The pictures, the smell of their clothes, even their personal products send memories flooding into a heart that is not nearly ready to let them go. It is not uncommon for the survivor to wear a sweater, jewelry, or spray the favorite cologne of the deceased just to have a point of connection or comfort. Be understanding and supportive of this process. These little things keep their mind stable as they pass through the changes of permanent loss they are experiencing. Remember, there is no rulebook on how to grieve. It's unique for every individual. We must never abandon a person in their time of greatest need and deepest sorrow.

I realized there were so many things going on in my head and heart; I was just trying to survive. I was experiencing the reality of death on a new scale. I was not prepared for this. I had to admit, I was broken.

The Lord shall preserve thy going out and thy coming in from this time forth, and even for evermore. Psalms 121: 8

PRAYER

Dear God,

As reality sets in help me to settle myself. This experience is mine, but everyone goes through something similar. I realize now that I am learning about compassion from my own experience. Even though I am still hurting, don't let me forget someone else is too. Help me to help them even if it is in some small way. It keeps me human. Walking with You truly has been a journey of self-discovery. You knew all along what I was made of. I just had to discover it for myself. This really hurts and it's confusing. I'm learning what it means to be honest with where I am. I'm hanging on to the little things because I can't let go, not just yet. I think I am starting to heal in small ways. I don't cry quite as much these days and I'm learning to talk to you regularly, like a friend should. Don't let my emotions die. Even though some of them may be of pain, joy still exists. It is something I will have to wait on. I really miss them in my life and I don't know that I'll ever get over that feeling. I know it takes time. Thanks for being patient while I go through these changes. Amen.

THOUGHT 8
When emotions die

There is no way at the time to know what will come out of your loss. Just take it one day at a time. Sometimes one moment at a time. There is so much you will learn during your process. Don't rush things. You are not as ready to move as fast as you think you are.

RESURRECTION

Out of death came something new. That's not always a positive thing. Knowledge and discovery come at a steep price sometimes. After many years I found myself just existing, not really living. It really is strange the way people begin to develop their own coping mechanisms; I was no different than anyone else.

Funerals had become so routine to me. Anytime you are constantly around something you can become immune to the normal effect it has on others that do not have to deal with it on a frequent basis. I wanted to feel something or anything. I had gotten so far out there I wasn't sure how to even begin to get back. During my journey of self-discovery, I found this: not only did my ability to feel sadness go dormant, but so did my ability to worship God.

> *"I wanted to feel something or anything. I had gotten so far out there I wasn't sure how to even begin to get back."*

The Bible says in John 4:23 (Amplified Version) *But a time is coming and is already here when the true worshipers will worship the Father in spirit [from the heart, the inner self] and in truth; for the Father seeks such people to be His worshipers.*

True worship is done with a healthy heart. I'm not talking about your physical flesh heart, but the place where your emotions live. A healthy heart allows you to connect to God in a wholesome way. When we worship, God loves to speak to our hearts; there is a precious wonderful time of peace and fellowship with Him. My heart had disconnected from viable emotions therefore, I struggled to "experience" the presence of God during my times of worship. I went through the motions that usually brought me close to God during my time of communion with Him. All I noticed was an obvious silence and feeling of disconnection from the life-giving source that

THOUGHT 8: WHEN EMOTIONS DIES

previously gave me so much comfort. I had no idea the side effect of shielding your heart from sorrow was closing it off from joy. I prayed and asked God to not let me live with a dead heart that separated me from experiencing the fullness of our relationship.

It is so important to have passion and emotions that keep you connected not only to God, but to others as well. I really didn't know how costly my request was. Sometimes, only experience can bring about necessary changes. It would take a deep emotional shock to bring my heart back into the rhythm of life. Had I known this, I would not have asked. The first emotion to violently awaken was sorrow. God knew it would take something deeply painful to break the stone from my heart and restore me. It wouldn't happen overnight. If I would allow my heart to submit to God's plan, it would begin to take shape. The shock of grief pounded my cold heart. It was a stabbing pain that there are no words for. The mission of restoration had begun.

A new heart also will I give you, and a new spirit will I put within you: and I will take away the stony heart out of your flesh, and I will give you an heart of flesh. Ezekiel 36:26 KJV

 **PRAYER**

Dear God,

This is so much harder than I imagined it would be now that it's my turn. I am learning how to submit and let You help me. I thought I was stronger than this, but as I let You in, I am finding more weakness than strength. I know it's okay to be sad. The sadness is actually helping me get through each moment because it's real too. I have to let it do the work it's meant to do inside of me. Some of the pressure is coming off and even though it's painful-at least I can feel something. I can't run from myself. Thanks for helping me cope. I have to remember You really do care and understand me. Amen.

THOUGHT 9
Caretaker for the wounded soul

Some things that happen in your life, you never saw coming. Just when you think you can make some sense out of it, things make a left turn and leave you at a dead end. When you get to that point, the best place to go, is to your knees. People are not God. Sometimes we are so desperate to talk to somebody, the person we choose doesn't have the answer we so desperately need. Keep in mind they could actually make things worse. I don't know about you, but I could do without the detour towards "worse."

REAL TALK

Hello sorrow. It's you again. Some days now are not good days. It is strange to know what sadness really is. It's starting to soak in. Sadness is when your heart cannot smile. Oh, my face doesn't show what my heart is feeling. I worry about the stigma attached to what I think this is. The simple things that gave me joy and purpose before are empty these days. I feel the sense of failure everywhere like a gray cloud that refuses to blow away. "Happy" is just an unrealized concept right now.

> *"When everybody thinks you're the strong one, nobody wants to listen when you try to tell them you are not alright."*

When everybody thinks you're the strong one, nobody wants to listen when you try to tell them you are not alright. They ignore what you say as if your words have no real weight. They judge how you are feeling by how you look outwardly. Maybe they don't know what to say; your weak moments may make them uncomfortable. The most crushing feeling is when you think you've found someone to reach out to only to discover, they too have major stuff going on in their life. You just can't bring yourself to lay any of your weight on them. So, you just pack your pain back into your bag and suffer in silence. Adding insult to injury, you find yourself encouraging them with words while you are on the brink of collapse yourself. This downward spiral comes from not using the biblical model for help.

James 5:16 (The Living Bible) *"Admit your faults to one another and pray for each other so that you may be healed. The earnest prayer of a righteous man has great power and wonderful results."* The most powerful thing about this is not one of us is perfect. We need each other. We have a habit of closing off from the real world so no one knows we are suffering. The voices we hear in the silence of privacy

THOUGHT 9: CARETAKER FOR THE WOUNDED SOUL

are often our emotions being influenced by the lack of fellowship of other people. Friends can offer good advice that can be very helpful when we are feeling abandoned by people who said they would be present after the condolences have died down. Healing can begin when we are willing to open up to another person that will not only pray but listen to our heart.

Words are powerful things, but they are even more powerful when we give them a voice to be heard. It frees us on the inside to release the pressure of negative thoughts and experiences. A true friend is willing to listen, even when you are just venting. They lean forward when you are talking, make eye contact and nod their head that says, "I hear you." Then, they repeat back what you said to make sure they understood you.

> *"A trusted, solid friend is critical to help you take intentional steps down the treacherous road to recovery."*

You must get your feelings out on the table so they can be lovingly understood and dealt with. Once the dialogue has begun, we discover the amazing power of agreeing in prayer for each other. Our focus rotates from being the victim to an active participant in our own recovery. The support of a solid voice can provide the flashlight that helps us navigate our way out of a dark place. A little light goes a long way. We can now officially begin the healing process because we have decided to stop hiding from the things that are tormenting us.

A trusted, solid friend is critical to help you take intentional steps down the treacherous road to recovery. Find that person who is willing to be your long-term care partner. This will take many days, many sessions, and lots of talking to God about what you are experiencing. Learning to trust "Him" with your treasured thoughts and emotions takes time and practice. God is waiting for us to get comfortable with our relationship with Him. He is patiently waiting as we creep slowly out of our dark spaces to share what is on our hearts. He won't leave you. He's not nervous about what you have to say.

I sought the Lord, *and he heard me, and delivered me from all my fears. Ps 34:4 KJV*

 **PRAYER**

Dear God,

I'm learning You have given us lots of answers. I may not always like the way You do things but when I really look closer, they make a lot of sense. I'm really trying to learn how to trust somebody and share what I'm really feeling, just like You said. Sometimes, that takes more courage than I have, but I'm starting slowly. Help me to find the right person to share my thoughts with in a safe, healthy relationship. I'm starting to see that others are a part of my healing too. I am so deeply hurt that even thinking about opening up my heart to someone is scary. I am just starting to tell You everything so I'm not sure about talking to anybody else about things. I know that I need to find someone soon and I will. Everybody needs somebody I guess. Thanks for helping me through these transitions. They are not easy, but I'm willing to try. Amen.

MY HEAD KNOWS IT

THOUGHT 10
Let's talk about the "D" word

I didn't realize there are so many that are hurting like me. We see them every day, yet they are invisible. Is it because it is easier to ignore people with issues we don't want to deal with? Maybe their pain reminds us of our own. Either way, they do exist! We must find a way to deal with the white elephants in the room.

IT'S REAL-EVEN IF NOBODY WANTS TO TALK ABOUT IT

There's a real community of silent sufferers. I wonder if the way we casually respond to their pain contributes to the wall they have built around their heart. After funeral services, people tend to return to their lives and forget about the people who have lost the most. I have found that it's not so easy for the victims of loss to return to their former lives. It is impossible. They are discovering and modifying how they live as well as how they think during this time of extreme change.

Suicidal ideation is common during this critical period. You may ask, "What is that?" Suicidal ideation refers to thinking about or planning suicide. Thoughts can range from creating a detailed plan to having a fleeting consideration. It does not include the final act of suicide. Christians don't think like that, right? Surprisingly, during times of mental stress or physical illness this is actually normal. When we are under extreme pressure from dealing with grief the thought of our death may seem like the answer to reunite us with the person we have lost. It is important to ask for help when dealing with these thoughts so they don't consume us to the point of action. Suicide is never the answer! You may need to seek the professional help of a counselor, psychiatrist, or pastor to get through this. There is no shame in getting help! Life is beautiful and you can get through this. You have value in this world; we need you.

As a friend, we must find a way, even if it is uncomfortable for us, to be a safe place of comfort and venting as others pass through their critical stages of grief. You may be the missing piece that helps someone survive their loss.

There comes a time when everyone needs someone. Tragic events affect us differently and we react differently. My husband lost his mother a few years ago. His reaction was to shut down. He is not emotionally expressive when he is suffering, so it was a challenge for me to dig deep to find out how he was really doing. I learned to observe changes in his behavior. I noticed the loss began to affect

THOUGHT 10: LET'S TALK ABOUT THE "D" WORD

the way he ate and the way he responded to people even asking him how he was taking the loss. I think we become weary of the same question from different people as if the sum of your life is your tragic loss. As it is, it's hard to move forward without people constantly ripping off the scab on your heart that is struggling to heal. My husband has been different since his mother passed away. He expends a lot of time and energy helping others. Sometimes too much time. For some, keeping busy is therapeutic. Serving others can give us a sense of purpose. This is good as long as it is not a cover for not dealing with deep seated, painful emotions and memories. It is healthy and normal to grieve. There is no normal timeline for grieving to conclude. Each person must go through their own process of recovery at their own pace.

I started to notice strange side effects in my life since my father died. Sometimes you think you are "normally" going through it, whatever that means. I put on the costume of externally looking okay but inside a storm was raging. The loss of my father gradually began to increase my sad days. Random thoughts and memories would torment my mind to the point I dreaded quiet times. My body began to react to the constant internal pressure. I couldn't eat anything without severe pain in my stomach. I had a dull headache most of the time; I was hardly sleeping at all. I went to my doctor to try to control some of the physical symptoms. After several medical tests, the pain in my stomach turned out to be ulcers. My blood pressure was out of control and my medication had to be changed several times to bring my levels out of the danger zone. I gained at least 25 pounds and my sleep pattern had changed. I was so tired all the time.

The responsibility I once loved of co-pastoring a church, I now despised! It was just one more group of people pulling on me to "perform." It didn't make me happy like it used to. Even the music I was passionate about became a drain on my life. It wasn't soothing my agony. No one was listening to me screaming, "I NEED A BREAK!" I was in a dangerous place emotionally. I am glad I did not lash out at people because I was frustrated. Grief comes to all of us in our lives. When a person is strong, be careful to listen to what they are NOT saying.

> *"When a person is strong, be careful to listen to what they are NOT saying."*

I know now this is called depression. It's one of those facts that Christians don't like to speak about. We are full of clichés and quotes from the Bible, but we tend to skirt around the issues that tackle people on the inside. Christians tend to think if they say the right scriptures and have faith then, poof—it's all good. My brain is full of those scriptures that have been infused into my life since I was a baby. I am familiar with the text and the passages. During that time, I struggled to find life from the pages. Comfort seemed to run away from me and rest was just an idea. This place of grief was unfamiliar to me. My head knows it, but my heart can't understand.

"And the peace of God, which passeth all understanding, shall keep your hearts and minds through Christ Jesus" Philippians 4:7 KJV

 **PRAYER**

Dear God,

I'm wrestling inside even though I look okay on the outside. Some days too much is going on in my head. I don't even know where to begin. My heart is a tangled mess of feelings and each day is a new struggle to begin again. There is no joy in the things that used to give me pleasure. I am so incredibly frustrated that no one is really listening to me. I don't even know what to do, and walking away doesn't seem to be an option. I really shouldn't be alone anyway. I confess, I can't do this without Your help. Help me not to pretend to be alright when I need help. Touch me on the inside where everything is so raw and help me to stabilize. There are so many questions and not enough answers right now. Help me to just hold on when I can't do anything else. I know things will get better but it's going to take time. Remind me again that You can do remarkable things in the right time. I'm holding on the best I can, and that's got to be enough. I'm just going to be still and wait on You. Thanks God.

MY HEAD KNOWS IT

THOUGHT 11
Nothing personal, just business

It's good to take time to think. When we learn to accept abnormalities in ourselves, we don't even notice them after enough time has passed. Dysfunction or no function can be seen as normal to us. It is never a quick process, but it is a consistent bruising of the soul until we no longer can feel what we should. Our emotions are an important piece of our construction. They protect us from collapse and provide an outlet of the pressure life produces.

As a Christian, you learn how to live your life according to the Bible. It is a great way to live and brings balance to gray areas in your life. Everything for me was going well. The church my husband and I pastored was growing. Our children were doing fine, and our marriage was thriving. The calling on the inside of me was strong. I felt as if that is what I was born to do. After years of pastoring, the inevitable happened; a member died. There is a different dynamic that happens inside your heart when a member of your congregation passes away. They are like your own children in many ways. Your mind causes you to reflect on all of the life events you walked them through. The memories of their early beginnings and their subsequent growth and maturity brings joy to your heart, knowing you played some part in their walk with the Lord. As a leader, you grieve in your own way.

It almost seems necessary to grieve in private because the members are naturally looking to you as their spiritual parents for strength and stability. It puts added pressure on an already difficult situation. You find yourself functioning on "auto-pilot," saying and doing all of the right things at the right time to make you appear more "pastoral." This type of performance-based acceptance causes you to put a lid on your own outlet of emotions. The frightening fact is, you push your humanity to the back and never really find the time to process your own personal grief. This is a recipe for an implosion from the time bomb of unresolved sorrow.

So, I began to push them down so far until they could not come out. I became robotic in my biblical responses to the cause and reason of death from what I thought was "God's point of view." I got lost in the fog called death and couldn't find my way back to humanity. Though the death of a member was hurtful, it wasn't a mortal wound to my spirit. I was able to keep enough distance from the pain of others to keep myself afloat on a life preserver in a raging sea. The pile of tears became a

THOUGHT 11: NOTHING PERSONAL, JUST BUSINESS

giant heap of hidden pain I was afraid to feel.

Life's wheels kept spinning and the cycle of loss continued several times. Here and there, members passed away. Again, I found myself handling the business of death the only way I knew how. The wall around my heart just got thicker and thicker. The only problem with building a wall around your heart is you keep the bad from getting in. Unfortunately, you also prevent yourself from getting out. On the exterior, I looked great! I appeared prosperous and happy but something had died inside. The numb feeling was not new to me.

Many years ago, I was a nurse at the Veteran's Hospital. I spent a lot of time on the medical-surgical unit, which housed some patients that were long term. As a nurse, you begin to grow somewhat attached to them which can be problematic (professionally speaking), when their health takes a turn for the worse. I quickly learned, in order to do my job well, I had to adapt to becoming detached. The death of my patient could not affect my professionalism. The same person I had cared for medically for weeks, was now deceased. I had to prepare their body for the morgue without being devastated.

The first time it happened, I was shaking inside. The body even smelled different when the life force was gone out of it. My co-worker carefully walked me through the end-of-life processing, checking off every box. I didn't want my co-worker to see me break, so I held it in. Nothing prepares you for the stark difference between life and the physical body after the living spirit has departed. I will never forget my first experience. The walk to the morgue was terrifying and lonely. I realized one day we would all end up that way—placed on a cold, metal tray with a tag on our toe. Then, stored in a refrigerator until the mortician arrives for our now empty flesh home.

As I locked the morgue door, I had a million thoughts running through my head. I don't remember much about the rest of that day. My mind and heart were forever changed. Nobody was leaving that room under their own power ever again.

I got through the hospital's protocols. They established a new normal for dealing with death. Loss became easier to process as time went on. After a while, I began to function pretty much on autopilot. When someone died, I didn't feel anything. I simply did my job with no connection. I walked each corpse to the morgue. I put them on the tray, closed the door and turned off the light. I felt my humanity slipping away. I realized that I needed to regain my emotional health. People wondered why I left such a wonderful, healing profession, but I knew it had changed me in a way I never expected. At that point, I stepped away from nursing for good.

Fast forward to today. I am a much older, experienced woman. Though I stepped away from nursing, I had brought the numbness along with me. I have seen so many things and experienced many more. There have been so many joys and sorrows along the way. I was

THOUGHT 11: NOTHING PERSONAL, JUST BUSINESS

able to absorb the joys to a certain extent and deal with the sorrows the best I could. I had no idea what was happening to my emotions during all of that. Inside I knew something was terribly different but I didn't know how to fix it. I felt as if I had seen and experienced the full range of life: from birth to death. I was rock solid. I really thought I was prepared, but I recently found a new place of sorrow that I had never faced before, not at this level.

My head knows it, but my heart can't understand it. Truthfully, I don't want to. "My head knowing it" refers to mental comprehension and the way we think. I was raised in the church so intellectually, I understand what the Bible says about life and death.

> *"There are so many scriptures that address these facts, but nothing really prepares you for the emotional toll when it happens up close and personal."*

When you read the accounts of what happens after life on this earth has concluded it makes everything pretty clear. You live your life in preparation to meet God at the end. It gives your existence purpose and meaning. There are so many scriptures that address these facts, but nothing really prepares you for the emotional toll when it happens up close and personal.

I could quote numerous scriptures without really thinking or connecting to them sincerely. That was my intellect kicking in. I had been raised hearing the Bible read and quoted since I was old enough to understand words. Knowledge can disconnect you from your feelings. Too much knowledge seems to be a type of teflon; nothing from life really sticks to you or gets in. It just slides off and you keep on going in your own direction. Nobody can tell you anything at that point because you think you already know it all. The scripture says, "The letter kills but the Spirit gives life" 2 Corinthians 3:6(b). What does that mean? You can be a smart dummy! Some people read just so they know a lot of facts to fight with. Knowledge that is used as a weapon destroys people and relationships. We can also get so deep into information that it begins to kill the faith-factor that allows us to believe God. True, we must do our research. Information is good when we use it in the proper context accompanied by our faith. Some things we learn from experience. There is no substitute for a first-hand testimony that gives credibility to your advice. Yet, there are other things that take some time but eventually we grasp the concept. When we put it all together, suddenly the light comes on! Now, we clearly see what existed all along. It's not that it wasn't there before. We were not at a point in our lives where we were ready to see it. Wisdom helps us know how to appropriate knowledge and when to apply concepts.

    We must have empathy for the plight of others. That's called compassion. With the feelings and the pressure that loss places in us, developing compassion for others is vital. Your heart is the seat of your emotions. It is such an important place that the Bible tells us to guard it. Proverbs 4:23 (KJV) *Keep thy heart with all diligence; for out*

THOUGHT 11: NOTHING PERSONAL, JUST BUSINESS

of it are the issues of life. In other words, take really good care of your heart because you use it to navigate your way through life.

Our emotions are difficult to navigate through because there are so many complicated areas that connect to each other. Just when you think you've got it together a memory shows up which in turn triggers the feelings that were associated with that memory.

The trigger can be the most random thing: a smell, a recipe, a place, a song, or a thought. When you lose the significant person who helped create those images in your life, grief shows up. Grief is a strong feeling of deep sorrow caused by someone's loss or death. I am discovering that grief never seems to be totally gone. It is just lingering in a different form waiting to surface again. You must learn to function in a new state of normal without that person physically in your life. You may find yourself wishing for one more moment or longing to hear their voice one more time. Emotional understanding comes from the heart not the head. "If my heart understands it, then it means I've accepted the loss and moved on. I know I'll get it eventually but who really knows when eventually is." Have you ever felt this way? I never really had, not to this degree, until now.

What caused this transition in my life you may ask? I suffered catastrophic loss 2 days in a row. The first loss was a dear friend who was like a daughter to me. She was the longest standing member at our church even though she was fairly young. We had been through so many life events together, both joys and sorrows. We had been singing together on our praise team for twenty-three years! She had become gravely ill. We watched and prayed as she slowly slipped away from us. At the same time, my father, (who had been seriously ill for the last three years) had taken a turn for the worse. I found myself going between two hospice facilities in the same week! I put on my pastoral face visiting my friend and my daughter face visiting my father. Both of these precious people lived less than a week. My friend passed on Saturday then my daddy passed on Sunday afternoon. I felt myself totally go numb. My brain went into a denial of sorts. I believe God was protecting me from a total mental breakdown. I cannot to this day understand how I made it through such a dark time in my life. The memories during the early days of this tragedy all seemed to run together in one big blur of sorrow.

 I went through such a confusing time both mentally and emotionally; I wasn't sure how to feel. Two deaths so incredibly close together were hard to manage in a healthy way. I didn't want the family of my friend to feel any offense because their loss was just as great as mine. For me, this meant two funerals were going to happen in the same week! This stretched me beyond comprehension. The mind however, is a powerful thing. I was able to be resilient, but it came at a terrible price.

 In the weeks following the loss our praise team sang on Sundays, I noticed the absence of her clear,

THOUGHT 11: NOTHING PERSONAL, JUST BUSINESS

beautiful soprano voice only to glance over at her vacant microphone and it would hurt all over again. I had to stand in a public place appearing strong while trying to avoid the open display of my crumbling heart. It made me wonder why her? why now? God, just why? We tend to ask many questions in these moments, but the answer never comes. Some things just never make sense in our minds or hearts. The struggle is real to find a praise to lift up to God in emotional places like these. Even though He is sovereign, we may question the justification of death that happens at seemingly the wrong time. It wounded my spirit to lose her. I felt the sadness and grief for her young daughter she left behind. I refused to be consumed by the swirl of emotions of her passing, so I just pushed them down with all of the other unresolved emotions from my life experiences. It was getting crowded in there.

I hated that my daddy slipped away, seemingly in a moment. I had been by his side all night. I stepped away for just a while just to take a little break from the pressure-packed situation called Hospice Care. During the small window of time that I was away, daddy slipped away peacefully. The reason I had stayed all night was I wanted to be there when he transitioned, but it didn't work out that way. I loved my daddy and he loved me. We had a wonderful relationship. We were so much alike in a lot of ways. As a pastor, he shielded us (as children) from a lot of things the best he could. He made my childhood magical and sweet. Losing him was excruciating. My father was very ill for the last three years of his life. I don't care how "prepared" you think you are for that moment when someone passes, you never really are.

While I was away at a conference three years prior, the message came to me in a dream. Three times the news came to me in a statement by random people saying, "You know your daddy died?" I awakened with dread and cried most of the day. I was trying to understand why God would do this. Why would He allow this? I struggled to come to grips with what I had clearly heard. All of my life I have been a dreamer. I understood the weight of this personal message from God. I sought out a counselor as I poured out my grief from the message. I knew it was serious. I knew it was real. I knew it was coming. After much prayer and struggle with the message, I realized how loving God was. He was preparing me ahead of time for an event I was not ready for at that time. After three years of waiting, I thought I had come to terms with my father leaving us because of his illness. When it happened, my world crashed. My heart, that was so hard before, found its heartbeat of emotion again. God, I know this is what I needed, but this is not how I wanted it to happen.

I will also put a new spirit in you to change your way of thinking. I will take out the heart of stone from your body and give you a tender, human heart. Ezekiel 36:26 ERV

# PRAYER

Dear God,

I'm starting to see something happen in me. I am becoming something new. I guess I was all along. That doesn't make this easier, just a little clearer. I'm sorry for my anger with You. I guess my anger is really pain that I'm expressing from my mouth. Really, that's what I think You want from me, expression. The more I hold on to stuff, the more it holds on to me. Now, I'm just kind of numb from it all. This loss is settling deep inside and I know it can't stay there. Learning to let go is hard because it means I need to actually trust You in this. If I really believe what I'm saying to You, it means I have to put actions with my words. I don't know that I'm totally ready for this, but I'm willing to try. I've got to start somewhere. I guess this is as good a time as any. I have no idea what I'm doing. I know I will stumble along the way. Please don't let me fall and hurt myself even worse! I want to finish what I have started so I can get some freedom. After my rant, I looked up and You were still there. I guess You really are a special Friend. Thanks for sticking around. Amen.

MY HEAD KNOWS IT

THOUGHT 12
Depression and religion don't mix

Finding comfort means knowing people don't always have the answers you need. It is okay to seek help outside your normal circle. People really do want to help. Find out where your help can be found in a community of support systems.

Recently, a new page of pain was navigated into my life. This was something I didn't want to ever feel, but I needed to know for myself. Somedays, I feel like I am riding the rapids on a home-made raft! At any minute, I could capsize and drown in the waves of misinformation! In my search for understanding of the place of emptiness called depression, I found religious misunderstanding.

What do I mean? Previously, I had mentioned my fear of judgement from the religious people. I found my fear to be surprisingly accurate. Depression is one of the taboo topics when it comes to the church. When I say the "church," I'm not talking about the building. I'm talking about the people. Religious people tend to imply that the suffering individual is at fault for their emotional struggles due to a lack of faith and prayer. Their sickness is perceived to be a badge of spiritual weakness. The church has a difficult time dealing with issues of the mind. I wonder if they can even comprehend the fact that what goes on in the mind needs as much healing and compassion as what goes on in the physical body. Again, religion tends to demonize the issues that involve the mind. Therefore, they don't have to be addressed. This creates a culture of silent suffering for fear of judgement from people we may look up to. Truthfully, it's not just religion that doesn't understand mental health, but the world in general. People who are suffering with challenges to their mental health are viewed as outside of what is seen as normal. We tend to struggle with an invisible sickness that affects the lives of people.

> *"Again, religion tends to demonize the issues that involve the mind. Therefore, they don't have to be addressed. This creates a culture of silent suffering for fear of judgement from people we may look up to."*

THOUGHT 12: DEPRESSION AND RELIGION DON'T MIX

Mental illness has been around a long time. I guess I really didn't realize how prevalent it is. As a child, I always saw people who were "different" in the church. They were a little off-centered in their behavior, but the church seemed to just accept them as part of the fabric of their quilt. Some of them hoarded things others had social fears, yet others had cognitive deficiencies in development, but they all were members of the church. There really was no intervention or assistance, they were just allowed to exist. Although they were different, I knew that God loved them just as much as He loved me. I saw their existence with others as normal.

As I began to process my recent grief, I came to a frightening conclusion. Something different was happening to me. No one could see it because I looked normal from the outside. I found myself in an extreme season of sadness. Not the type where you never smiled, but the kind that something in your heart never felt happy. No matter what I did, that nagging sense of despair just reappeared. I couldn't shake it or walk away from it. My every thought was consumed by the loss of my dad. The haunting memories that used to bring me joy only made me want to cry and scream. I felt so alone, as if I was the only Christian going through this. It made me feel like everything I was doing was just running on automatic pilot with no feelings attached. I just couldn't come out of it no matter how hard I tried. I was falling into the pit of depression. I really had no idea how to get out. It was swallowing me internally and I felt a new sense of panic. I began to search for a lifeline from a "seasoned" voice, a person who is not a novice, to throw me a life preserver as I began to sink. As I was internally gasping for air, they threw me a boulder!

Depression is a powerful downward spiral if it is not properly addressed. Depression does not discriminate! It affects the young, middle aged, and elderly populations. If we are truthful and examine our life's history, we will discover those extended periods of sadness were actually seasons of depression.

Many suffer silently because they are afraid of the judgment of others who do not understand it is a disease process. Our society has a history of making light of issues that are not easily understood. Recently, mental health has come to the forefront because of the confession of high-profile athletes dealing with dark tunnels of depression The lack of concern or taunting from misinformed people only increase the feelings of anxiety and loneliness the sufferer is experiencing. Hopelessness soon follows and suicidal ideations (thoughts of suicide) may creep to the surface. Just the thought of not experiencing the torment of emotional pain can be enough to tip a person's reasoning towards suicide. All that needs to happen is the slightest push from crass people to tip them over the edge of contemplation to decision. Words are powerful; they can heal or kill.

Mental health demands as much attention and support as physical health. Youth today are especially vulnerable to these low emotional points because they have limited life experience to navigate through these feelings. Often the despair of hopelessness and lack of professional support leads them to intense suicidal thoughts that require immediate intervention. Unfortunately, suicidal ideation is not limited to youth, but adults also experience the weight of despair that drives them to end their life prematurely. If we look closer, their symptoms were crying out for help all along. Nobody was listening for the silent scream. We only laughed at what we did not understand was someone's personal hell. I ask myself, "Have I ever been the one that pushed too hard?" My heart is sad and my head is beginning to understand.

    I previously stated that we could be so desperate for a voice that we can choose a person that makes it worse. Unfortunately, as I searched for solid answers, a person I trusted threw me a big rock! I heard this leader characterize a Christian suffering with depression as no longer useful in the Kingdom! No longer useful? When those words hit me, they cut me in a wounded place! I couldn't breathe. I expected some words of wisdom or solace, but the weight of those negative words on my desperate soul were shocking. Nothing hurts worse than when you are silently screaming, asking for help, and the voice you are trusting in (for some kind of hope) comes back with condemnation for being human.

    The worst answer you can give a person is a religious one. It comes from the self-imposed power position of looking down on people and speaking at them, not lifting them. These toxic words are void of compassion because they are spoken from a lack of personal experience. Too often we don't develop a soft spot for these issues until they affect our friend, our family or us directly. This is not a Christian perspective of unconditional love. I shouldn't have to hurt like you before I can have understanding and hurt with you.

Tomorrow, you may need the same compassion you neglected to share. I needed a reassuring Word of God's divine comfort to ease my distress, even for a moment. I found myself scrambling to shake the incompetent judgement placed upon people in my condition, so I could survive another day of my battle with sadness. I searched for personal definition. "Am I useless?" "Is God really finished with me?" I heard a whisper of "No," in my spirit. It was small, calm, and familiar. I knew in that moment, that the Holy Spirit was comforting me when I needed Him the most. We must be careful who we admire and the words that they dispense in our lives. If they hold too much power over us, they can destroy us with their words. It is important to seek validation from God because He alone knows who we really are. What happened to faith for healing or even listening to a person's heart even when it is uncomfortable to hear? That's like telling a person not to jump off a cliff while you are pushing them to the edge! Then while looking over at the wreckage of their lives you say, "Wow, I can't believe they jumped!"

The church must be a part of the solution, not an

THOUGHT 12: DEPRESSION AND RELIGION DON'T MIX

added weight to the problem. This is why the Word of God can't just be about religion. Religion sanitizes the user to make them appear righteous in the eyes of people. Religion should provide a system of operation, but it must be about relationship. Others may interpret the Bible in a way that makes them a super-person, without flaw or weakness.

On the contrary, the Bible is meant to be the life-guide to help us navigate through anything that may happen to us while we are here on earth. God knows we are flawed. He loved us enough to send Jesus to redeem us and the Bible to provide an understanding of His will for us. When we don't apply it correctly, it can be a cocktail of poison that is bitter to swallow, ugly to look at, and unattainable to the common person. God never meant distance from Him, but to close the gap and draw us closer to His love.

The last thing a person needs to hear in their moment of crisis is a personal opinion, especially if you are a leader. People are the most vulnerable when they are suffering. Your words of judgment may be just enough to crush any hope of recovery. Negative words and concepts tend to be amplified in the ear of the sufferer. The lack of true compassion is clearly conveyed as a person speaks with arrogance to a griever. God can show you sometimes better than He can teach you. People who judge others harshly that are suffering mentally, should be cautious. Religious people tend to speak from the "if it was me" perspective. The truth is, no one truly knows what they would do in any given circumstance until they walk through the emotions and pain personally.

The Bible does say you reap what you sow. Religious short comings should never dictate how we choose to help others. If we are lacking in an area, God will supply sufficient experience. Don't allow your judgment to cause God to change your tune by force because now it is your turn to suffer!

I am glad that I have a personal history with God my Father and I know He loves me. The Holy Spirit has been my Comforter and Stabilizer during this terrible season I am in. My prayer is that I can learn from this place my heart is in so I can help others heal. I know I must help myself first before I can truly help someone else. This is a time to guard my heart, for out of it comes the issues of life. I cannot allow words spoken in ignorance to pierce my faith. God has a divine purpose even in all of this. I am glad I have enough foundation to drown out careless words that should never be heard by a hurting soul. My head knows it, but my heart is struggling to understand how people can be so cruel.

Everything in the world is about to be wrapped up, so take nothing for granted. Stay wide-awake in prayer. Most of all, love each other as if your life depended on it. Love makes up for practically anything. Be quick to give a meal to the hungry, a bed to the homeless—cheerfully. Be generous with the different things God gave you, passing them around so all get in on it: if words, let it be God's words; if help, let it be God's hearty help. That way, God's bright

THOUGHT 12: DEPRESSION AND RELIGION DON'T MIX

presence will be evident in everything through Jesus, and he'll get all the credit as the One mighty in everything—encores to the end of time.

1 Peter 4:7-11 MSG

PRAYER

Dear God,

I don't know everything, but I do know You love me. My struggle to smile again is real and sometimes I feel like I'm not sure I will ever be happy again. This gray place is frightening to me, but I know even in here You are here too. It is a comfort to know you are everywhere I am. I'm asking you to just protect my heart from hatred, my mind from crazy thoughts and hold my soul in Your hands as I make my way through this. Cover my heart and shield my ears from hearing things that don't help me. Help me to shake words off that cut me and allow Your grace to heal me in those area that are tender. Protect me from anyone or anything that would harm me. Give me peace in my mind and allow me to rest when I lay down at night. I need to be built back up in places where I feel low. Help me find the help I need and allow me to make it through each day with Your help. I'm holding on to what I know to be true and consistent. That is, You love me more than I can understand. You have never left me by myself. I'll take each day as it comes and trust You to hold my hand. Thank You God for loving me through this. I'm not going to let go of You. You are my helper. Amen.

MY HEAD KNOWS IT

THOUGHT 13
Precious memories, Amazing grace, and Tears

When I decide I am ready to see clearer, God will begin to show me what I never understood before. I am discovering my human side, which doesn't make me any less of a Christian, it makes me more. It takes a lifetime of varied experiences to make you a complete person. Some of the hardest times of my life filled in some gaps in my vision of the human experience. I once was blind, but now, I'm starting to see.

3/22/19 - What a tough week.

It was the one-year anniversary of my dad's passing away. Funny, people call it transitioning, but it's death, hard and simple. You feel it in your gut. It stays on your mind. The moment the calendar hit March, I started feeling the stress. My mind reminded me of what happened. Sleep began to fade night after night. I could not rest and barely ate. My heart had physical pain that I can't quite put into words.

The mental pressure is a whole different issue that I struggle to explain to people. No matter how well I attempt to describe it with words, there is no substitute for actually walking through a personal experience with loss. I have found others struggle to truly understand the concept of invisible pain. Your mind is the most powerful part of you. It drives your life and dictates your day. When grief grips you, it's hard to shake. I have been around grief but never has it touched me this close.

I loved my daddy. He was a truly amazing man. He made me feel safe and valuable. He was the first man I ever loved. He was such a mild-mannered, quiet person, always the peacemaker in tense situations. He always seemed to know what to do, when to do it, and what to say. I watched him tip down to the basement to his prayer room way back in the corner. I remember sneaking down there when he was gone just to see what was so special about that room. I remember the special paneling with raised diamond shapes carved all in it and the room smelled like cedar and olive oil. It was full of books for reading and meditation and a desk and a comfortable chair. My dad spent a lot of time talking to God, and God talked to him. My dad had a way of talking that let you know he measured every word he said to you, because it had value. Slow, deliberate, yet loving. He connected to my heart and our spirits were similar. We would sit in a room, watching boxing on tv and not have to say a word to each other. I watched his boyish grin during those famous bouts only to later discover that when he

THOUGHT 13: PRECIOUS MEMORIES AND AMAZING GRACE

was young, he wanted to be a boxer. Neither of us was a person of many words in private settings. He would always pat my head and tell me he loved me. I watched this man go to work every day at 6 am, come home, then turn right around and serve people in his congregation and the community. Most of all, I admired the same man I saw at home was the same man I saw at church. He was never in a scandal, never spiteful, and never harsh. He was always calm in the face of fire, and one of the best preachers and teachers I have ever seen. As a result of the life he lived in front of me, I searched for those same qualities in the man that would be my spouse.

Everyone who met my dad loved and respected him. When he died, I didn't realize how hard it would be to let go of him. He was entwined around my heart. Memories that people tell you to dwell on, only made it more painful. I have driven past my childhood home too many times. These memories are sweet; my heart longs to go back to a time when life was simple. When you realize who you lost, you struggle. I feel the effects of grief some days more than others.

It's a strange thing to know death and the finality of a loved one leaving you. The bigger mystery is for your heart to try to heal and identify with what you know. Seems like the two just can't connect. I don't know that you ever really recover. I think you learn to live with your new normal. I hope that as each year passes, the pain will begin to be less. It's not that I love him any less or miss him any less, I am just learning to cope a little more. I am

MY HEAD KNOWS IT

sure the small things that remind me of him will make me smile sometimes, laugh sometimes, and cry sometimes. My head knows it, but my heart can't understand how to recover from this huge void in my life. God, help my heart to heal, day by day.

I'm learning more about myself each day and how to walk each step with the Lord. Sometimes you think you really know yourself until something major happens. It is at those times that you struggle to find your foundation when it feels like everything is shaken. I'm finding you can be shaken to your core, yet not destroyed. Though I am struggling through these days I know I am never alone. I understand that all things work together for good, even when they are devastating at the time. That's the logical side of me that helps me cope.

One day it will be easier, just not now. I'm learning to accept the Lord's timing and wait for healing to come. Miracles are instant; healings take time and occur gradually. This whole grief thing is a healing process. So, until my healing is complete, I will wait patiently on the Lord and take away another life-lesson that will help someone else. Our lives are not always about us, but rather learning to endure hardness as a good soldier of Jesus Christ and embrace our moments of humanity. Even Jesus wept. I've discovered that this little Bible verse, as a matter of fact the shortest verse in the Bible, has a powerful meaning. Let's revisit this point.

Jesus, the Son of God, knew that in a few moments

THOUGHT 13: PRECIOUS MEMORIES AND AMAZING GRACE

He was going to raise His dear friend Lazarus from the dead. Yet, the reaction of His arrival at his gravesite was, He wept. People observing this occurrence said, "Oh, how He loved him," after watching Jesus weep so heavily at the tomb. It speaks to human issues and emotions of dealing with the grief process. Imagine the emotional pressure of the scrutiny of Martha stating, "If only You had been here, he would not have died." Even though Jesus was the Son of God, He was in the flesh, having the human experience called life. Jesus had a new vantage point of grieving the loss of a loved one that had died. There was a new agony in His heart that reflects the pain we feel even today when someone close to us dies. It was necessary for Jesus to experience all points of the life we live.

The simple statement of the fact that Jesus wept at Lazarus' tomb releases us to grieve. Tears are a natural, spontaneous release of emotional pressure in the grieving process. They are bigger than just God having something to bottle up! Tears have incredible value. There are different types of tears. Tears that are shed out of emotion, tears that are produced as a natural protection of the eye, and tears that are excreted due to irritation. Let's talk about emotional tears for a moment.

The tears of emotion, especially from grief and loss are incredibly therapeutic. They allow the emotion to come out of the body in a physically evident form. It is dangerous when you can't cry. Inadvertently, this has happened to me. People call it being strong. There is something about seeing another person cry that affects the

MY HEAD KNOWS IT

watcher.

A series of tragic events began to occur in my life. It seemed to be a season of one thing after another tearing at the fabric of my soul. The climax at the time was the death of my mother-in-law.

> *"I found myself asking God to help me release the pressure of grief by crying. Tears have great value especially to me."*

She had become such a critical piece in my life I really couldn't let her death soak in, I wouldn't. She had been there when I needed her so badly and I felt so connected to her. She emotionally rescued me in a time of great suffering. I held on to her in my heart to help me heal in some raw areas where I was torn up by life. When she died, my heart safety net suddenly ended. "What will I do now?" I felt the emptiness and panic in a new way. I knew what was supposed to happen as I stood at her casket, but it didn't. What was going on? I couldn't cry. I needed to, but the tears just wouldn't come. Was it a fear that if I started crying, I would not be able to stop? I felt the clog in my heart that stayed with me long after that moment. After that, several other important people in my life passed and still no tears. I found myself asking God to help me release the pressure of grief by crying. Tears have great value especially to me.

Tears that are a natural protection to the eye have no emotion attached. They just flow and do their job, which is to keep the eye moisturized and clean so it can function. There are even artificial tears you can purchase

THOUGHT 13: PRECIOUS MEMORIES AND AMAZING GRACE

if your eye ducts are dysfunctional. We cannot not survive without tears. There are times when natural tears keep our hearts covered spiritually. I have had instances where tears are spontaneously flowing when I am not feeling happy or sad. They are a protection of sorts ensuring the process of crying still functions.

Other tears are to wash away things that are irritants in the eye. Irritants can be microscopic, yet the body immediately recognizes the intruder and begins to produce tears to wash it away. There are times when we spend time with God that tears symbolically occur as a sign of a deeper washing spiritually. As we submit our emotions to God, He allows us to experience the brokenness that tears bring. A spontaneous cleansing occurs that keeps our heart pure before Him. In essence, these three types of tears have value and keep us in health physically, mentally and spiritually.

It has been a little while since my dad has passed, and I still struggle with the release of tears. I know that it should happen because it's normal. Maybe I'm in fear of what people will think, or how it may affect them if I start crying.

Leaders affect people without even really trying. Everything they do is observed and interpreted by others. If depression pulls hard on me and I stop functioning in a leadership capacity, how does that affect others? I wonder if this is the reason why I buffer my pain. I know I am human but somehow, I feel responsible as others view how I handle my grief. I recognize my heart is hurting, but my outer shell doesn't show it. I can still do all of the things I normally do out of habit. This can affect not only my ability to grieve, but all areas that God touches that involve how I feel. Excessive sadness can alter my heart towards worship, love, and passion.

That is a dangerous place to be. It gets easier to remain closed off to emotions. The longer you wait to address the problem the harder it gets to open up. Healing really needs to occur. Internal pressure must be released. You must find a place alone so you can cry.

My head knows it, but my heart can't understand that releasing these tears to God is normal and necessary. God, open our emotions so You can heal them.

He will wipe every tear from their eyes. There will be no more death or mourning or crying or pain, for the old order of things has passed away. Revelation 21:4 NIV

THOUGHT 13: PRECIOUS MEMORIES AND AMAZING GRACE

 **PRAYER**

Dear God,

Here I am again, today in a little different place. I don't know how I can feel numb and pain all at the same time! I'm so bottled up with thoughts and emotions that I just feel lost. My head says one thing, but my heart is dealing with something else. I'm so tired, exhausted really. I feel like I'm fighting myself. I just want to be normal, whatever that is. It's one of those days that I don't know exactly what to ask for, so I'll just ask for help. I never thought I needed to cry but I know now I do. Help me find time to just spend with You so I can get my head in the right place. This is harder than I thought it would be. Please help my heart to begin to heal. It's so torn up by my grief. I know You are listening. Thanks for that. Amen.

MY HEAD KNOWS IT

THOUGHT 14
The season for me—time

You can be with someone and yet alone. No person can really know your internal struggles, but God does. As we begin to understand ourselves, we become open to accepting our strengths and weaknesses. God can only help if we are willing to admit we don't have it all together. There is a time and a season for everything that occurs. Sometimes, it's just my turn. I'm learning how to handle my seasons, with God's help.

Today more than ever I know that I have met depression, face to face. The constant, nagging heartache that doesn't go away. The struggle to smile, laugh or just feel happy isn't made up. It's real! I used to think you can just decide to be happy and poof, you're happy. The battlefield really is in the mind. I've tried to tell others about how this really feels. I have never seen so many Christians brush off what I am trying to say! I get quick evaluations and short answers that make no sense. I realize there are times when your heart needs to be heard to be able to heal. People don't always have the capacity to handle the pain you feel because they are accustomed to leaning on you. I have been trying to step away from all of the duties I perform to find personal time to heal. I realize that people are used to taking and not giving. Every time I begin, someone cuts me off, and I just shut it down.

I hope that if you are experiencing despair that you seek out help. It will not get better just retreating from life. It can become a vicious, seemingly hopeless cycle. There must be a time of retreat where you take time out from your duties so someone can help you. It is important to operate from a position of strength and wholeness. Serving others can feel therapeutic at the time, but it is only a temporary buffer against deep agony. You can only pour from what you have inside. Don't pour from an empty place! You will eventually realize all you gave away you needed for yourself. Some places, only God can quench the dryness and fill the empty hurt you feel. Recovery cannot effectively begin until you stop doing so much for others and begin to find the me-time that helps you rediscover your life after loss.

In all the confusion that loss brings, I have begun to discover the power that is in the Word of God, not just what I've read, but what it has been speaking to me.

To everything there is a season, and a time to every purpose under the heaven: A time to be born, and a time to die; a time to plant, and a time to pluck up that which is planted; A time to kill, and a time to

THOUGHT 14: THE SEASON FOR ME-TIME

heal; a time to break down, and a time to build up; A time to weep, and a time to laugh; a time to mourn, and a time to dance;

Ecclesiastes 3:1-4 KJV

Everything in life has a season. There will be a time for all of these things to occur. Some of them are cause for celebration and the others pull at the painful places. God is in the middle of every season we walk through and He alone can help because He knows us in a way no one else does. I found myself crying out to God, "Help me in this season!" The cry is not always tears or yelling. Sometimes it is the smallest of whispers or the inaudible voice of my heart pleading to my God for His help. I discovered the place of healing is a private audience with Him alone where He can deal with the wholistic person. If you are busy all the time, maybe you are avoiding alone-time with yourself and God. He's waiting in the place you're running from. It's time to stop running away from Him and run to Him.

> *"Everything in life has a season."*

But I have prayed for thee, that thy faith fail not: and when thou art converted, strengthen thy brethren. Luke 22:32 KJV

 # PRAYER

Dear God,
I am praying today because I'm learning so much about myself and others. I want to move on, but I'm realizing it's not time for that. Help me to take time out from everyone and everything that seem to pull on my attention and focus on myself. It's hard because it makes me feel selfish. Help me not to look at all the things I do well without thinking about it. Automatic pilot is not helping me deal with my issues. I guess it is my time for just me and getting better. During all of this, I still am holding on to my faith because You are the only thing that is solid right now. It is going to take a while. I know all of me can't get fixed overnight, but I am willing to acknowledge I am not okay. God, this hurts more than what I thought. I'm running back to the One that can truly help me. It's You God. Thank You for helping me see I need to take time to deal with my season of grief. It really is a slow process. With Your help, I can do this. Amen.

THOUGHT 15
Family feud

Getting stronger means something needs to get challenged. Physical workouts often cause soreness because the muscles haven't been used for a while. You first will have extreme soreness because your muscles are basically torn down before they begin to build up. If you can endure the painful season strength will begin to show up and eventually not hurt quite so much. My heart must be getting stronger because right now it is a painful season.

We are all working towards a goal. The truth is, we are never perfect. Some of us have old ways and thought processes that should have changed by now, but we keep them as an "untouchable pet." Yet, with the same mouth we are quick to judge others. Our faith in Christ allows us to receive eternal life, yet there is internal work to be done. Our ways must change to Christian standards. Too often, we bring our "old ways" into the church-life without converting. We are not truly ready to strengthen others until we handle our "stuff." Freedom is available to everyone, but can only be received by confessing there is a problem. Grief often reveals problems that have not been previously resolved. Families may have horrible outbursts that can even lead to physical altercations over unresolved issues. Emotions are raw and tension is high. It is a great time for self-examination. You may find that the problem is not with other people, but the true enemy lies within you. You cannot be your best self until God deals with all of you. It's me oh Lord-help me so I will be fit to encourage and strengthen others, even in my pain. Remind me not to hurt others because I am hurting. Pray for a spirit of refreshing to wash away any sediment that is not useful in your life.

The finality of death leaves many things unsaid and undone. Often, family dysfunction is amplified when someone dies. I remember a funeral director telling me they actually had to break up family fights at the funeral! Coming together to put on a show of unity is common. Appearances are everything because no one wants to make a bad showing for everyone to see. This only adds to the complicated grieving process and often pulls families further apart. Private messes remain and family members separate and return to their lives until the next time something happens. Without a mediator it is difficult to heal even though it is a perfect opportunity to do so. Feelings are often raw and boil to the top. Unfiltered words spew out as grief gives people permission to vent. When we learn to have real conversations about things

THOUGHT 15: FAMILY FEUD

that matter, we can make progress. We may find it is past time to finally resolve our long-standing issues with each other so we can be whole again. It is just a beginning and dialogue must continue to get the best results. We must be willing to forgive and establish a renewed relationship. Nothing that has happened in the past can be changed, but we can change where we go from here. We must ask, "What is our motivation?" Are we trying to win an argument or solve a problem? You can win and still lose. Forgiveness may be one-sided if the other person has not arrived at the decision to move forward. It doesn't mean you forget but it does mean you choose to let go of the pain that was caused. Every person has made mistakes in their lives. Death is final so why not use the finality of the unchangeable to change what has great potential to be fixed? We are still here. Let's write a different future to our family story.

> *"The finality of death leaves many things unsaid and undone."*

Create in me a clean heart, O God; and renew a right spirit within me. Psalms 51:10

PRAYER

Dear God,

In my recovery process, I realize there is so much more I haven't dealt with. My grief has just brought everything else to the light. While I'm dealing with my grief, I might as well address anything else that is holding back my complete healing. I don't want to walk out of this just better, but whole. I ask You to show me any secret thing inside of me that has been a hinderance in my life. Don't let me be afraid to change. I know it's never too late. I'm learning how to let go and forgive, maybe not all at once, but little by little. This is the perfect time to grow in some areas I have let change the person you meant me to be. I don't want to cause anyone pain because of things I do or say. Please forgive me for stuff I have let get to me and take my peace away. Most of all in the end, I know I will have to answer to You for the life I have lived. All of this clarity really hurts. Help me to deal with what I see in a healthy way. I know, if I am honest with You God, my strength will come. Help me to continue what we have begun. Amen.

THOUGHT 16
Where do I go from here?

There are lulls when you feel like yourself again. These reprieves are temporary because God knows how much we can handle at one time. He allows us to experience what our life can be like after our intense season of mourning is over. In the middle of the active times, we may wonder what to do next. There are so many directions we can go, but it is critical we choose the right one. Often, the wrong path leads us into a relapse of pain. It may feel like the loss just occurred again! It is okay to not be "yourself" for quite some time. Your emotional health is the most important thing. There is nothing pleasant about coming face to face with your pain.

This is a question that comes up so quickly. Some try to pick up the pieces prematurely and move on only to discover they were fractured in places they didn't even know about yet. It is human nature to survive mentally and physically. Before you launch out on your big journey to live, realize you may not even truly know where "here" is right now. Miracles are instant. Healing however takes time. Real healing is slow, methodical steps towards progress. The steps may be small, but they are measurable. It may be difficult to accept that you need down time after your loss. The times of silence are the most difficult to deal with. Your ears search for the sound of your loved one that is now absent. Each day becomes a new challenge to accept that the empty place will never be filled. Little reminders crop up in unexpected moments and you struggle once again to process your grief. Some days you can reason and pray your way through. Other days you are overcome with tears and wild emotional swings of all kinds. All of this is normal. It takes a lot of time to settle into a place that becomes "here." Some may ask, "Well, how long does that take?"

It is different for each person. A sudden, unexpected loss may leave you swirling for a long time. You have had no warning to even prepare mentally for the permanent departure of someone from your life. Chronic or terminal illness affords you time to contemplate the real possibility of someone dying, not that it is any easier to lose them, you just had some sense of knowing beforehand. Either way, you must process your loss.

It is okay to be angry, sad, tearful, confused, lonely, frustrated, fearful, and unsure of the future. Don't look for people to give you permission to grieve. They may not understand your reactions or delayed grief long after the funeral is over. They can simply return to their life as it was before. You must process the hole in your soul

THOUGHT 16: WHERE DO I GO FROM HERE?

and find a place where healing can begin. Your loss will forever change you. Nobody tells you that. It is alright to be changed from who you were. This is the beginning of the discovery of where "here" is.

Don't be in such a rush to impress people. Sometimes we try to look strong for others. I call that "pouring from empty." The tendency is to try to go back to who you were, doing the same things, maybe even taking on a cause or two. These things can be premature if you haven't dealt truly with yourself yet. Moving too fast will cause meltdowns because one of those reminders showed up and you simply were not prepared for it to hit you that way. Those moments knock you to your knees and cause you to retreat from life for a while. Just because you believe you've processed your grief don't think that it won't happen to you. It can. I have days that are pretty good, but then there are others that a simple pleasant memory that floats through my mind deeply cuts my heart. I feel the tears welling up and a fountain of grief takes a grip on me. I say to myself, "It is normal to miss him and it's okay, even healing, to cry." My head is starting to know it, and my heart is beginning to understand.

> *"Moving too fast will cause meltdowns because one of those reminders showed up and you simply were not prepared for it to hit you that way. Those moments knock you to your knees and cause you to retreat from life for a while."*

For in much wisdom is much grief: and he that increaseth knowledge increaseth sorrow. Ecclesiastes 1:18 KJV

PRAYER

Dear God,

I am coming to You again for our time together. There are days that are really great, but then there are days that are really rotten. On my good days I feel like I have really made good progress. On my difficult days I realize that real healing takes a lifetime. I can see now that I moved too quickly in some areas and I paid for it! I'm not superhuman. I shouldn't expect too much from myself and I need to give myself permission to properly grieve. If I don't, I will keep cycling around this same issue until I get it right. I am learning so much about myself and yes, it has come at a terrible price. The lessons however, are priceless and I will never forget the seasons I am journeying through with You. I really want to thank You for Your love and patience with me. I didn't think it would be this intense, but anything worth having takes work. My relationship with You, Father God has developed in a new direction. For that alone, I'm grateful. Talk to You again soon. Amen.

THOUGHT 17
Help me!

Grief is one of the most misunderstood emotions. Maybe because it is so complex people don't even try. It is difficult to make the right decisions because most of us have not had any formal training in loss. Grief is bigger than just loss of life. We can also experience loss of safety, security, innocence, hope, peace, and so many things we haven't even thought about. Finding help can be complicated. Some want to maintain their image of strength and needing help projects an image of weakness in their evaluation.

HELP ME

The words I hear the most are help me. Nothing in life prepares you for the valley of loss. It is truly something that must be experienced personally to be understood. Knowing and understanding are two different concepts. Knowing is more of an intellectual process. Understanding is empathy because you have felt something similar person who is suffering. Help comes from a good friend who knows how to listen. It is true, you may not know exactly what to do or say, but you do know how to listen. Make eye contact with the person that is speaking, even if it is uncomfortable for you. Remember, they need your help. It is not about you right now. Lean in towards them and nod your head to reaffirm you are really listening to their heart. Pray for their comfort, protection, and healing.

> *"People may forget what you say but they never forget how you made them feel."*

When a person is at the peak of grief, their mind and heart are wide open to all sorts of attacks. The last thing they are thinking about is protecting themselves. People have the tendency to do and say all sorts of things, some very foolish. They may make suggestions that are not wise or say things that may be cutting or insensitive. You must guard the grieving heart from mortal blows that may come from people that are close to them. When people are in crisis negative events are amplified. The person may have meant no harm, but their actions may leave a horrible scar to a hurting person. Maya Angelo said, "People may forget what you say but they never forget how you made them feel."

When you are addressing a grieving person, always take time to measure your words. Ask yourself, "How would I feel if you said that to me right now?" Resist the urge to compare your time of loss with theirs. It will never, ever be the same. Loss is a personal experience.

THOUGHT 17: HELP ME!

Every person's heart feels differently about the same event. It is not your time to tell your story unless they ask. I've watched a grieving person almost be put in the position of the therapist for someone else because they were laying their story out in living color. The look of confusion on their face devastated me! It said, "I can't believe you're saying this to me right now while I'm in crisis!" What made it even worse was this person was considered by others to be an expert with loss. Moments like these leave a scar. Never marginalize anyone. Make their voice valuable. If they trust you enough to speak to you, you must be careful to listen. It is a serious thing to walk through dark places with someone. A good, solid friend is invaluable. The mourner will find their way, but it will take time. In critical moments, your presence in the room can be enough to reassure the griever.

It may not be the right time to intervene by doing things for the person. Grievers need the most care after the hype of the early days have passed. Everyone has gone back to their lives while the grieving person is just starting to realize what they need. Where are all of those offers for help now? We are quick to move on not understanding our most effective time is after others have gone. Make yourself available and accessible to the person when they request time with you. Their heart is grasping for help.

From the end of the earth will I cry unto thee, when my heart is overwhelmed: lead me to the rock that is higher than I.
Psalm 61:2 KJV

 **PRAYER**

Dear God,

I'm crying out to you for help! My heart gets overwhelmed with all of this. I don't know what to do. I feel the panic in my heart. I don't feel like I'm trusting You. Reassure me that it's going to be alright. I'm going to stop struggling with this and learn how to rest in You. I realize that means I must stop trying to understand this and trust your decisions. Worrying about it can't change the outcome. I need to learn how to live again. That means I also must learn how to heal. You alone have the peace I need so I will patiently wait as You work things out for me. Thank You God, Amen.

(For the friend) Dear God,

I recognize at this very moment I can do something to help. Remind me to be your hands and ears as my friend goes through this. Help me to give a sense of comfort and stability when everything is turned upside down. This is hard, but I'm willing to extend myself to just be there. Help me to say and do the right things at the right time, Amen.

THOUGHT 18
The morning after

The blur of celebrations after a loss feels like a huge responsibility. It is. I mean let's be honest. A person's life is reduced to that final moment of reflection and then their life is neatly packed away. You want the celebration to represent who the person was in this life, which is an impossible task. There is no way to condense their existence into a fleeting moment. When all of the crowds of people go away, you are left with yourself. They pack away the commemorative t-shirts, release the balloons, blow out their candles and move on. The shock comes when you realize how easily the "professional mourners" move on to the next event and you are struggling with a lack of support and an empty life. Definitely not what I expected.

There is always a morning after a big event, loss, or celebration. Realize that the sun will rise tomorrow. We have to make decisions today that concern tomorrow. It takes a clear head and a clear heart to make solid choices that are not based in necessity or emotion. We cannot continue to wallow in the jaws of grief indefinitely. There is a set season for that, but after the season has ended, it is time to live. What you do the day after testifies to the day before?! When these events happen, we proclaim on that day that the event changed us and we are going to do better, be better, but what about the morning after? Most often we regress back to our old nature because it is easier to just go with the flow rather than push to make changes. We must intentionally move toward the direction of healing and freedom. Maybe you need to find that time to truly grieve the loss of someone. Give yourself permission to miss somebody and plenty of time for reflection. It is part of the life cycle. People often quickly develop an outlet for their grief rather than process it. They form foundations and lobby for causes in the name of the person just to feel better. The energy we pour into our new passion may eventually run low and we meet our grief once again face to face. Sooner or later, we have to deal with our loss in a healthy way. If we don't it can destroy us mentally and physically.

 Jesus did a monumental thing when He rose again on resurrection morning. He gave us the power to change and live a new life, but only if you want it enough to accept it. Who are you today, the old you or the new you? Realize that random waves of grief will still show up from time to time. You are human. Take the time to address the human side of you also. Embrace the power of each moment as God allows you to experience the loss.

THOUGHT 18: THE MORNING AFTER

Precious memories, how they linger. It won't always feel like this. Life will have times of joy also. It is alright to let the rawness of your loss begin to heal. As you journey through this you may find a new sense of guilt because the grief is not as strong as it was previously. God has begun to take the raw edges of your loss and carefully stitch them back together again. He applies healing ointment that begins to soothe the touchy areas that need more attention as the weeks pass.

> *"Realize that random waves of grief will still show up from time to time."*

God provides a filter that eventually takes the awful sting from death and comforts us with His Holy Spirit. We begin to grieve "differently." We recognize the emptiness from our loved one that has departed this life, but we can also rise up the next day and live. The journey is now leading us to the place called acceptance.

*I said, L*ORD*, be merciful unto me: heal my soul; Psalm 41:4(a) KJV*

PRAYER

Dear God,

Thank You for our journey this far. I have grown in unexpected ways. I realize that this grief process is my journey alone. I never knew the grief I walked through would mature me in so many ways. I don't know everything, but I do know that I am better than when I started. This is a new walk with You. I have learned so much about You and even more about myself. I am starting to feel new life rising up inside. My life does have more chapters to be written now that I know You better. Thank You for helping my head to comprehend the things I thought I already knew. My heart is coming to a place of acceptance and healing. The tears are a lot less than before though I still have sad days. Losing someone is never easy. I believe I can see the sun peeking through my clouds. I think I'm going to be alright in time. Thank You for being with me through all of this. Amen.

THOUGHT 19
Acceptance

Sooner or later, I need to put away the tissue, get up off the couch and find my life again. It doesn't happen quickly, but it does happen. Nobody said this was easy or simple. There were days where I didn't want to live anymore just because it hurt so bad! Those are the intense moments that will pass in time. The realization that others have moved on means that eventually I must make decisions that help me go forward also. It is a place of maturity, helping me grow up in areas that were small. My personal development in my walk with loss is full of ebbs and flows. Long as I take positive steps, no matter how small, that's progress. Every season takes time and God gives us grace for each one we travel through. We have to remember to give ourselves that same grace to flow with the seasons.

Every season takes time and God gives us grace for each one we travel through. We have to remember to give ourselves that same grace to flow with the seasons.

This may be the most difficult point to arrive at. It doesn't mean you agree with the death, but you have come to a point where you are truly ready to establish a forward trajectory. Moving on doesn't mean you have forgotten the person. It means you realize you still have life to live. There will always be some sadness in your heart. You wouldn't be human without it. This is your new normal. However, you may discover strength comes from surviving the common foe, death.

We realize they will never return to the earth and every moment we spent with them was valuable. A monumental point of acceptance arrives when you can think on the good memories with joy rather than tears. People tend to rush to get to this stage because they worry others will think their grief period has taken an excessive amount of time. Appearances often dictate how we handle our time alone with our pain. There is so much pressure on us to move on and rejoin the land of the living. The change in our perspective of life has been modified and we are learning to walk with a new view of life.

There are many things we learn as we take this new journey. Unfortunately, only experience can teach them to us. We may discover that we have become teachers rather than students. The best teachers have traveled the road they are guiding others on. Pain does have a purpose and there is a season to everything we go through. Compassion finds a new home in our heart. We can now operate out of empathy, not just sympathy. As we watch others navigate the same path we have journeyed, our

THOUGHT 19: ACCEPTANCE

hearts hurt a little-maybe a lot. In the early stages, we may avoid situations that pull at the scab of healing that has started to form on our hearts. Watching others travail in grief may be too difficult to bear at first. I know people that would not attend any funerals in the early stages of their own personal loss because emotionally, they simply could not bear the pain. Watching others grieve may elicit floods of negative memories of their own intense process with death.

We understand that death comes to everyone's door. The residue it leaves may not be immediately evident. We can sincerely pray for them in the dark days to come as the reality of life after the funeral sinks in. Given time, the manifestation of the side-effects of loss may become clearer and people need help dealing with them. We discover humanity experiences the same emotions and weight, but with the help of God we can also find relief.

> *"Moving on doesn't mean you have forgotten the person."*

This is where the scriptures come to life. They are not some magic charms that we can quote and "poof," they work. The power of the Bible begins to take shape in our hearts when we receive it as truth, even when our head can't wrap itself around the whirlwind of death. We must begin with our head understanding and eventually our heart will follow.

Meditation is a good way to be alone with your

thoughts and God's Word. Take more time to read the Bible. Find specific passages that stand out to you and think about them. Go for a walk or ride. Play soft music as you concentrate on yourself. Write down the passages that stand out to you so you can remember them. God loves these times of fellowship with you. Your mind needs this time to diffuse the tension and pressure that you experience.

Yet there is one ray of hope: his compassion never ends. It is only the Lord's mercies that have kept us from complete destruction. Great is his faithfulness; his loving-kindness begins afresh each day. Lamentations 3:21-23 TLB

PRAYER

Dear God,

I'm learning slowly how to be grateful for the small stuff. I woke up this morning and took a breath. That was an accomplishment in itself. You know the journey I have been on. I'm not going to lie, it has been more than I can take some days. The more I read the Bible, the more I'm getting to know You and myself. I don't understand all of it, but there are certain parts that really have helped me. You said each day is fresh and You are there waiting for me. I really need You to be there. I'm making steps-some forward some backward, but I'm still moving. I'm asking for just enough strength and courage to get through today. I don't know what's waiting for me, but I can find comfort because I understand You know what is ahead. Thanks for being consistent. I am changing and growing each day. I really hope this grief will get better in time. I know I can trust You with all of me. Amen.

MY HEAD KNOWS IT

THOUGHT 20
Auto-pilot moments

I never knew how many things I could do without even thinking about it. After my loss, I started to evaluate the things I was doing for other people. Most of them made me feel useful, but it was really an easy way of avoiding dealing with the issues I had hidden deep inside. Until you really are better you may be doing more harm than good.

Remember, give yourself time to heal. That means lots of time, days, weeks, months, even years. Even after you consider yourself to be healed your human side may still have auto-pilot reactions. Things may happen that you really can't control. I will use myself as an example.

Now it is coming up on the second anniversary of my father's death. Last year was much harder. It was all so fresh to me and my soul longed just to hear his voice. Some days I felt like I was going to lose my mind. God held me together. I thought I had reached a new level of recovery. I felt strong and had returned to some of the duties in the church I once enjoyed. I was finding my spiritual stride again. Then the strangest thing happened, as soon as the calendar hit March. Sleep immediately left me. I started being up later and waking earlier. At first, I was confused as to what was going on. I thought maybe I needed to pray for someone else or God was speaking to me.

After I thought about it, I realized it was my subconscious reaction to the upcoming anniversary. Nobody tells you these things. It was an automatic reaction. Deep in the recesses of my mind, was grief. My heart was still struggling with the terrible loss even though my logic was processing my new normal. As the actual day draws closer, my mind finds a way to count down to that moment of loss. I am giving myself permission this year to be human and miss him yet again. It doesn't matter who can't understand why I am still crying and my heart aches again. This part of my recovery and others have experienced the same thing. This process called healing is more complicated than I ever imagined. Take the necessary time to help yourself before you try to help

> "*Slow progress is lasting progress.*"

THOUGHT 20: AUTO PILOT MOMENTS

others. Slow progress is lasting progress. Rapid ascent leads to deadly crashes!

The signs may not be the same for you but trust me, you will remember. Don't beat yourself up about it. You may think you are not progressing as far and as fast as you think you should have by now. There is no time limit on grief. This truly is part of the ongoing process of releasing your pain. It can not be ignored or pressed into a little container to be stored on a shelf. The body tends to relieve itself of internal pressure by expressing compressed grief. It is a healthy thing to give your emotions space, safe space for expression. Some people visit the grave of their loved one. Others cannot relive the experience of the cemetery. Both are healthy because they are individual choices. Taking time for self-care is critical to your healing process. Do what fits your emotional frame, not others. Your mental wellness cannot be ignored. We are complicated creations. We exercise our body, but our mental health is often dismissed. Time to grieve will be necessary for a while as our minds and hearts release the pain of permanent loss. There will come a time that the intensity of these moments will soften when you can still function during the anniversary of your loss. Give yourself permission to be human and take time to respect your own personal space of grieving.

Peace I leave with you, my peace I give unto you: not as the world giveth, give I unto you. Let not your heart be troubled, neither let it be afraid. John 14:27

PRAYER

Dear God,

Today, I am in an unexpected place. I'm sad again. I really thought we had made great progress. I was getting back to my routine and then I got hit with the anniversary. I didn't want to feel this way again, but I do. My patience is short with others and I find myself retreating from people. I just want the sadness to go away. I guess I don't want to hurt like this. I'm trying not to miss them, but I do. God help me during these days to give this pain to You too. I realize I'm human and this is taking more time than I wanted to admit. This grieving is a heavy thing to work through, so I am letting it out. Free my heart from this pain and trade my pain for Your peace once again. I do see it is a little easier than last time. Thank You for being so patient and understanding with me. I guess I don't know myself as well as I thought I did. I need some more time and that is okay. You love me just like I am. Thanks God, Amen.

THOUGHT 21
Loss is bigger than death

Death is different for everyone, yet the same. When closure is stripped away it is difficult to find the moment to say goodbye. It is critical to our emotional and spiritual health to have time to let go of people that have died, especially when it was sudden or unexpected. Covid made sure we all felt loss.

The year 2020 ushered in a new year with a vengeance. A pandemic swiftly struck the world and COVID-19 raised its ugly head. No one in the entire world was prepared for the destruction and side-effects from this virus. In just a few months it crossed ethnic, racial, and cultural lines that spanned the globe. It was especially hard on those of us that reside in the United States of America. We have grown so accustomed to so many rights and freedoms that are automatically given as a citizen here. With the exception of the 911 attacks, America has been shielded from the world's sufferings. When mandates were issued and "stay at home orders" were given out, many Americans felt the borders of free choice close in on them. This was a new concept, to have our choices made for us. Our security of our safe, free, secure life was lost. The reality of our mortality was shoved in our face. We became helpless victims to a disease we could not see or feel until it had gripped us. Seemingly in a moment, our powerful machine of modern medicine was helpless to save us from falling prey to a ruthless enemy. The angel of death began to sweep over our elderly, teens, children, and seemingly healthy middle-aged adults. Worst of all, it removed the ability to physically touch another person or even be in the room when they died. To add insult to our injury, we also could not attend the funerals to say a final farewell due to founded fear of exposure and contamination to a virus they could neither cure nor vaccinate against.

Every one of us seem to know someone that has suffered great loss from COVID-19. Our hearts reach out in sympathy for them because our hands cannot touch them. Our minds cannot grasp the sheer numbers. Millions have died as our uncertainty rages on. Some bodies were quickly reduced to dust or buried rapidly as morticians hit the breaking point because they were overwhelmed with the massive, rapid losses of life. I have watched America become numb to the constant stream of victims from this horrible pandemic. Even some that survived COVID-19 live each day with the residual side-

THOUGHT 21: LOSS IS BIGGER THAN DEATH

effects of the disease, further adding to the syndrome of loss of life as they knew it. We began to shield our hearts from the deadly enemy of loss that no one could control. Our emotions grew cold towards each other's losses and Covid deaths became "normal."

Support groups are absent during this time as people focus on their own survival. Others have experienced overload as they pretend none of this is happening. They were determined to recover our lives as they used to be, knowing deep down inside nothing will ever be like it was before we were all touched.

They live in ways that are a risk to themselves and others. Now, we have an entire generation of people who will need mental and emotional support. They do not know how to release a new level of grief and loss of so many things. The side-effects have not yet peaked from the trauma of such a great sudden loss to so many families, churches, schools, co-workers, and society in general. We have gone into survival mode, not really addressing the underlying issues because there simply is not time. We have focused on trying to recapture a "normal" life, ignoring the risk of certain exposure to a formidable enemy that continues to kill despite our best efforts. The arguments continue over the true effectiveness of vaccines and the possibility of lasting consequences in the absence of long-term studies.

I struggle now as I see the heroes on the front line of healthcare battle every day to stay ahead of the virus.

A new variant constantly forms further complicating our fight. As we spiral yet again into the next outbreak, I pray for the medical teams that are exhausted and overwhelmed. Our medical facilities are a constant hub of activity, leaning towards capacity with those that are desperately ill. It has raged on longer than anyone anticipated, and we do not yet see and end in sight. Unfortunately, our survival mechanism has kicked in, and we are numb with the daily news of bad news. People have begun to act like the pandemic does not exist simply because they can no longer cope with the morbidity of our once impenetrable lives.

> *"Have I sympathized with the sorrow of others?"*

We must examine our emotions. What has this really done to me? How has loss affected my grief process? Have I really accepted the loss of people and life around me? Have I sympathized with the sorrow of others?

These things keep us human and are part of the life cycle. I cannot fully address this syndrome because we have not yet begun to recover from this horrible disease. I am sure the fall out will be evident in the years to come. All we can do currently is pray for God's covering over our lives and hearts as we slowly walk through our loss of innocence and normalcy.

This is a new syndrome of grief without closure. My head sincerely knows it, and my heart cannot begin to

THOUGHT 21: LOSS IS BIGGER THAN DEATH

understand the void of fellowship and support during this catastrophic, universal loss.

Don't fear, because I am with you; don't be afraid, for I am your God. I will strengthen you, I will surely help you; I will hold you with my righteous strong hand. Isaiah 41:10 CEB

PRAYER

Dear God,

Today, there is so much fear and so much loss. We have lost things we couldn't have imagined in our lifetime. The disease has taken away our sense of peace and security. Our children live in fear. We don't know where to turn. We cannot solve this alone. We ask for Your loving arms to surround us during this time. Heal broken hearts and wounded minds. Help us to run to You when we have nowhere else to go. In Your arms is peace and safety. Heal our minds, bodies, and spirit as we continue to fight just to survive this time in our history. Remind us to love each other and be patient. We are all suffering in one way or another. We have all lost something. Amen.

MY HEAD KNOWS IT

THOUGHT 22
Healing for the grief that suddenly found me

Nobody wakes up knowing that things will drastically change in an unexpected way. The worst feeling is when the time comes when you are totally unaware that you just had your last moment with someone special.

It hits...suddenly. Your mind does not operate in the defensive mode because there is no reason to. When the news grabs your heart, your mind struggles to process what just happened. Death makes no appointments with any of us, it just shows up at its appointed time. It's never the right time especially when it's someone young and vibrant. I questioned why it happened. Could death have been prevented? I wondered how death affected the loved ones closest to the person when the news hit them. My mind visualizes the screams and the shock and the incredible grief that the body can't endure. I know the numbness of denial. The tender areas of my heart begin to pound with empathy, understanding to some level the loss, but knowing I can never personally experience the depth of agony they are going through at that moment.

Suddenly, everything just changes. It is impossible to know what we should say or do in the immediate situation. It is a good time to be available and listen. Comfort is hard to find because nothing will make it better or change what is. The person is forever gone. Only their personal items remain to speak to us about the life they lived. Slowly it will begin to set in that they will never return home to us again. The empty silence is the worst because it confirms the reality of death.

Unfortunately, I don't know all the answers. I do know the loss of a loved one hurts worse than anything I've ever felt in my life! I truly wish no one ever had to experience it. Unfortunately, death is one thing that ties us together in a common experience. The only thing that changes is how it happens.

Once you learn how to truly pray and talk to God, it really helps you heal. He never expects us to be perfect but transparent. The secret pain we keep can make us sick. When you go to the doctor it does no good to lie about what is really going on in your body. You are the only one that truly knows what is happening inside. The doctor can only make a proper diagnosis and prescribe the correct treatment if he has full disclosure from us. Though it

THOUGHT 22: HEALING FOR THE GRIEF ME

may be uncomfortable to tell everything to them, it is critical to our recovery process. The physicians have had years of extensive education and training so nothing we say can really shock them. The fear of being judged can stop us from getting exactly what we need. God is the same way. He is the Creator of every living thing. He knows all the intimate details about us. If we ever want to recover from the pain of grief, we must be open and honest with the Great Physician-God. Jehovah Rapha-the God that heals. I don't think we understand the access we have to His office anytime we need a visit. Grief crisis moments can happen at any time day or night. It's good to know God is always on-call, waiting for a healing visit in his office. He never judges us for being human. When we expose our wounded heart to His hands amazing things can happen.

> *"Suddenly, everything just changes."*

We can never make progress if we don't utilize the resources that are available to help. People are one of God's greatest gifts. Even just a friend that listens when you are falling apart is invaluable! Venting is an important step when things bubble to the surface. A hug can be food for the soul. There is no substitute for the human touch. Compassion is a necessary gift that is meant to be shared with every one that is suffering. One day, it will be your turn either to give or receive this gift.

As the daggers of loss come and go in your life, it is critical that you take time to process and begin healing to whatever degree is possible. The road to recovery is a long journey full of hills and valleys. You may feel that your progress is going great, and then loss again punches you in the gut! At that moment you discover areas that still need some attention.

It is important when engaging a grieving person to share, but not project your pain on the other person. The goal is to help them survive their current experience. Your history of loss will assist you in understanding the range of emotions and behaviors you may see manifesting.

Meanwhile, the moment we get tired in the waiting, God's Spirit is right alongside helping us along. If we don't know how or what to pray, it doesn't matter. He does our praying in and for us, making prayer out of our wordless sighs, our aching groans. He knows us far better than we know ourselves. Romans 8:26-27 MSG

PRAYER

Dear God,

I know the days have been harder than what I ever imagined. I'm just asking for a little grace to make it through today. I believe it is a progressive thing. I can't get it together all at once, so I'll settle for just today. Help me to be okay with missing someone because that's natural. I don't need to be strong for anybody else. Help me to simply find the strength for me. This time, I need it the most. Talking to You about the deep things I have hidden is new for me. I am scared to begin to open-up emotionally about the things I've tucked away. There is so much in the closet of my heart that I must begin to let You see. I do want to heal. I realize that You understand my fear and apprehension of letting others into my heart's circle. You are sending people in my life that will understand where I am. Show me what I need to do to start getting better. Amen.

MY HEAD KNOWS IT

THOUGHT 23
The costume of strength

The worst feeling in the world is to know every eye is looking at you when you're barely keeping it together. It just adds to the pressure of navigating through grief.

The greatest pressure of all comes from others that are viewing your grief experience from the outside. I'll never forget the processional up to my father's casket for the last view. You can feel the eyes glaring at your family, but your sunglasses hide the windows of your battered soul. If you are unfortunate enough to be related to a public figure, there are unspoken expectations of behavior that prevent your grief from being expressed. Part of me wanted to crumble as I took those last steps down the aisle but then the other part of me didn't want to give any satisfaction to the professional mourners that were waiting for that moment of weakness. It is a vicious circle that steals the humanity of a torn heart. If Jesus was the measurement of that pressure-packed moment, then I failed miserably! Jesus was able to release the pressure in bitter tears at the tomb of Lazarus, in spite of all of the onlookers expecting to see Him in professional form. For me, another blow to my injured emotions meant more work I would need to do later on. Grief lurks in shadows waiting to remind you that you have not dealt with it.

Grief doesn't have a consistent frame; it just modifies to whatever space it can fit in. It is our job to recognize it when it shows up and take time out of our busy lives to process it. Putting on the costume of being the strong one doesn't make you strong. It exposes your weakness of not being able to release your grief which is toxic to the soul. The poison called sorrow has to be expressed to be removed from the body. Sometimes the fear of others seeing your open grief drives you to close off any expression of sadness.

I have heard clear instructions to "be strong" as if an open display of sorrow will destroy your reputation. The words linger as you struggle to press down the explosion of unimaginable loss, just for the funeral. You may feel that you survived the critical moment of the service, but the manifestation of grief will return. When we don't allow grief to surface, it begins to cause confusing side effects that we may not recognize as

THOUGHT 23: THE COSTUME OF STRENGTH

connected to our loss. Going on with our lives may lose its energy and we may begin to struggle with our purpose for continuing. In the early days and months our every thought may be consumed by loss, becoming a recurring daily theme. People may see us as chronically morbid as we obsessively focus on loss. We may become angry if others cannot see our viewpoint or they have simply grown tired of the same topic.

Relationships easily erode at this point as we shift the blame of our lack of recovery on others inability to understand what we are really going through. Though we may not have clearly communicated our struggle we expect our friends and family to be "mind readers." When everyone is not immediately in agreement we lash out, attacking their lack of sympathy for our journey, forgetting none of us are experts in this area. Every person is responsible for dealing with their own grief. That may look different for each person. What works for me may not work for you. What is important, is that we do work on it and not just sweep grief under the rug.

God is understanding of our journey in accepting the loss of people in our lives. We are the only ones that are really shocked by how painful it really is. The work of coping with death is long and tedious. We can all heal to a degree, but it does take time to address things as they surface. You will always miss them. You wouldn't be human if you didn't. However, there is life after death, emotionally and spiritually.

If we give ourselves the grace to hurt, we give ourselves the grace to heal. They go hand in hand. Hurting comes before healing. The problem with squashing the hurt is it makes no room to heal. Be patient with your emotions and allow them time to recover. You cannot just pick up where you left off and pretend none of this ever occurred! That is a fairytale with a sad ending. When you come to yourself, you will realize you attempted to move forward too quickly without dealing with the baggage that came with the experience.

> *"Life is full of twists, turns, and unexpected things."*

Our humanity demands moments of expression so our body can operate the way God intended it to. Grieving is a natural process that has a place in our lives too. If we allow patience to have her perfect work (James 1:4), we can see the rainbow of promise begin to shine again in our lives. After the dark storm of loss, the sun will return. Understand, it will feel different because you have emerged different, but you emerged.

My head knows it, but my heart can't understand the end of life that always feels sudden. I always feel like there was more I wanted to say or more I wanted to do. I look back at wasted opportunities when I should have just enjoyed the moment. No matter how great the memories I can still see how it could have been better. That's humanity, the 20/20 vision in our rear-view mirror. These can be the silent battles of guilt in our mind as we struggle to let go of what we can no longer change. I keep

THOUGHT 23: THE COSTUME OF STRENGTH

speaking to my head so it can begin to grasp forgiveness for all of the things I didn't do right and allow my heart to receive God's unconditional love. He knows our faults and insecurities about the unknown, yet He is passionately in love with us.

As we feel healing begin to show up, we must allow it to happen. When God closes a chapter in our life, we must stop sticking our finger in the book trying to find the page. When it is time, it is okay to move forward. You will never forget them.

Life is full of twists, turns, and unexpected things. It's not so much that they happen, but how you choose to handle them that determines your character. Time is short. That fact is never clearer than when you lose someone.

My head knows now, more than before this difficult experience occurred and my heart now can understand I must go on. I'm learning how to live again, and just maybe I can help someone else that is just beginning their process.

A glad heart makes a happy face; a broken heart crushes the spirit. Proverbs 15:13 NLT

 **PRAYER**

Dear God,

It's me again. I feel different than when we first started talking about this. I know that there will yet be challenges ahead. I also know I can talk to You whenever I need to. Thanks for being so patient while I'm figuring things out. My heart stings at times, but I now know it's because You're still working on some issues in me. Sometimes I'm doing pretty good, other days I just can't get it all together. I know I'm growing little by little, but I really wish it could happen all at once. I am so tired of thinking about this every day. My head may say some things, but my heart now knows that You love me. We are getting through this together. Thanks for holding my heart while I work this out. You have been such a faithful friend. I can depend on You, always. Amen.

THOUGHT 24
Battered, Bruised, Blessed
Sometimes the pain of the process doesn't make sense to us, until later!

Sometimes, the glory of something doesn't show until after the process is complete. Some say a green banana is full of potential or the yellow ones are perfect. Nobody wants the black ones which were also once full of potential and perfect. Now, are battered, bruised-seemingly beyond use from wear, tear, and simply waiting. What man counts as past the prime God evaluates as "fit for use." There are things we can only learn through life experiences. You see, until we are tested and weathered by life, we have no real credibility. The trials that God allows should make you better, not bitter. Even in your bruised state a few more things may come along that break you down. Just know you are never alone. The final product... is glorious. Now out of those black bananas comes this perfect banana bread. Sweet, warm, glorious, resurrected to a new life to be broken again for many. Three bananas can feed three, but how many can this loaf bless? Thank You, God, for this life lesson. When you learn to just tell God "Thank You," then you will discover the wisdom of His plan. Nobody says His plan is easy, but it is the right one for your life.

I know God has a really large bottle for all my tears. My journey has been watered with lots of them. I have cried about a lot of things, but the death of my father really broke and battered my soul. If we knew what we would have to go through for God to use us, would we still say, "yes?"

I am starting to see the fruit of God's divine wisdom in this process. Healing and restoration have begun to take place in my family that I never thought I would see. He is delivering me from deep seeded fear and removing the root of the need for acceptance. The cost was almost more than I could bear, but God knows the hearts of us all. We must be willing to offer God absolute surrender of our lives to see His will truly manifest in us.

Without my pain I could not and should not pen this book, but God knew what it took for these words to come to life. Through all the brokenness I am learning to just tell Him "Thank You." It doesn't have to make sense to my mind. My heart knows how much He loves me. I am learning to tap into the potential that was given to me to help someone else. Just know in this journey you are not alone. Each stage of grief is unique for each person's life. Do what you must to get to the next stage, but whatever you do, don't quit. You can make it through this with God's help. There is purpose in every tear and every prayer.

> *"I know God has a really large bottle for all my tears."*

You may ask the question "Why?" and truthfully the answer may never come, at least not the one we want to accept. Death does change us all. It changes people around us. Death may reveal hurtful truths we did not want to face or believe existed. Death causes us to see the value of a life well lived because we really don't know how much time we have. Some things are only revealed to us through hard experiences. God is there to help us process these times and help us to be truly whole. It will take a lot of time as we work our way through. In the end, the lessons we take away are priceless.

If your heart is broken, you'll find GOD right there; if you're kicked in the gut, he'll help you catch your breath. Psalm 34:18 MSG

 **PRAYER**

Dear God,

This is a tough place for me to be. I am shattered by so much loss. It even hurts to breathe. Don't ask me to see the good in this because I don't. Nobody should have to go through pain like this! The agony is more than I can stand. I'm talking to You because I need somebody to hear my pain. I'm confused and lost. This is just not a good time for me. They said You pick up broken pieces, well I've got lots of them. Please help me to just make it one more moment. This broken place is dark and lonely. Truthfully, I'm glad nobody else can see it right now. You're working on something in me. I don't know what it is but I'm saying I trust You with it. I don't understand it, I don't want it right now, but You're all I've got. I guess You know what to do. I'm trusting You with issues and feelings I can't even begin to understand. Help me make it through this broken place. Thanks for listening. We'll talk again real soon. Amen.

THOUGHT 25
Finally!

When you find your design and learn to walk in it, it's everything! It's life to your soul and spirit because you have discovered what God meant when He made you. Embrace your ideas, creativity and skill. God is standing up and saying, "Finally, they get it."

As the moments turn into days, days eventually into months then months stretch to years the pain dulls a bit, except for those pangs of anguish in unexpected moments. God really can do the impossible if we are willing to become part of His plan.

Our lives are really a vapor that seem to evaporate so quickly we regret any of it we wasted. As I reviewed my life, I began to take a hard look at how much of it was wasted on self-pity and blame shifting. You may ask yourself, "What is blame shifting?" Well, it is an emotionally abusive tactic or behavior. The person has difficulty accepting responsibility for their own problem, so they project the blame on others. The person deceives themselves and has great difficulty even seeing themselves as the great part of the issue. It takes an awakening of reality to bring a person out of this state. I really thought the anguish I endured was something that needed an apology from others so I could be healed. In reality, I needed to release others from the prison I put them in mentally so I could be set free from the effects. I alone was responsible for holding on to my misery.

Walking through this extreme grief process began to tear down idols I had erected in my heart. You may ask, "What is an idol?" Idols are something that holds a value to you or is revered, almost worshiped as untouchable in your eyes. For me, my personal idols became so large, the love of God and His principles could not penetrate their cold shadow. I did not see the bitterness that had grown from a root to a strong cedar tree. My badge of persecution that I wore seemed to be a constant Memorial Day of all I had suffered in this battle called life. I wasn't living, just existing.

When my daddy passed, the power of my idols started to fade, and all I wanted was real healing.

THOUGHT 25: FINALLY

I started to see that I had no right to linger in bitter moments of things that were lost and relationships that were crucified in my past. I looked closer at the false perceptions and lies that flourished which caused a spiritual cancer. It slowly ate away at my relationships, emotions, and family. There comes a point in time when we must take responsibility for what we have allowed to control us. There is no freedom in choosing to remain the constant victim. We have to decide we have had enough. Yes, a huge wall began to crumble that day my dad took his last breath. I evaluated myself. "Is this all there is? Is this God's best for me?" These were the hard questions that needed truthful introspection-no time left for games.

I decided I had let bitterness and pride take too much away from me. So, many years lost to hatred and misunderstanding really made me angry, but what was I going to do? The answer was simple, but not easy. I had to allow God into my heart to heal me so I could heal others. My healing meant I had to die, not physically, but emotionally and mentally. I had to stop thinking so much and defending my feelings and do it the way God commanded. Total surrenderance is a hard thing to do when you think you've got it all under control.

> "Forgiveness is not an emotion; it's a choice."

Forgiveness is not an emotion; it's a choice. You decide to let things go and let people into your life and heart. If you wait until you feel like it, it will never happen. Let's face facts. The more you ruminate (or deeply think and meditate on events) the harder it gets to find the emotion of forgiveness. The wounds are raw and you refuse to allow the Holy Spirit to comfort and do the work of sewing your raw edges together so they will heal and eventually be whole and functional again. Anger and bitterness are easy seeds to grow during this thought process, yet they are a nightmare to remove once you let them take root. They are like dandelions at the surface. You can pull them up at the top and think they are destroyed, but until you pull the root, given the right circumstance and just a little space of opportunity, they return.

The moments that you will experience can provide opportunities of deep healing as you process your loss. Make no mistake, you must take the time to process what the loss means to you then find the life that comes from it. Allow it to focus you again. You...are still here, living even though it is different now. Don't let their life and death be a vain moment. Find true purpose in it.

I stopped making excuses for what could not be done and stepped over that line. Was it hard? YES! Was it necessary? YES! The death brought life and hope to my broken spirit. I found a reason to love and reach out again. I laid down my history of pain and loss. I embraced the fact that I cannot change what has already occurred. I cannot bring back the things I lost or time I wasted, but I can change how I live going forward.

True forgiveness is what I decided to offer others.

THOUGHT 25: FINALLY

Not the conditional kind that offers reconciliation at a price of partial distance, but the kind that opens my heart to be vulnerable again because that's what Jesus paid for, complete healing.

I'm just beginning on this road and yes there are bumps along the way. When I hit them, I allow the Holy Spirit to dig up the ruts in my road and do "quick repairs" so I don't regress. To my amazement, I am beginning to see changes I thought were long gone. My heart leaps in hope once again that God is truly the restorer of things that I once counted as destroyed and lost forever. The Bible is not a book of suggestions. It is a life-changing book of principles for successful living. For it to work, we have to follow the guidelines, especially when we don't particularly agree with what it is asking of us. Remember change begins one step at a time based on your decision to heal. Stop waiting for the feeling to arrive. Just do what will start the recovery process. The rest will happen in time.

While finishing this book my mommy passed away. Once again, a flood of emotions devastated my life. This time though, I feel different. There are still rushes of intense waves of grief when I see her pictures, or I visit some of her favorite places. I appreciate all the memories she wrote on the pages of my life. There are days when I laugh at some of the things she used to say and other days I cry because I just miss her presence. I often think about just how proud she would be if she could see all the things her children are doing right now. I have moments where

MY HEAD KNOWS IT

I get overwhelmed. I know when it's time to step away and cry the moment out. It's really healing to my hurting soul...and totally normal. Though I'm hurting, I'm finally learning how to walk through the phases of my grief.

It is strange when both of your parents are gone. You may feel like an orphan. Parents seem to ground you no matter how old you are. I am learning to trust God to fill the gaps and keep my heart protected.

This cycle of death and grief is part of life. Finally, I am learning how to accept them as they arrive individually and give each occurrence the proper space to be refined.

My head knows the Word of God and now, my heart is beginning to conform and understand God's loving plan for me.

The Spirit of the Lord is upon me, because he hath anointed me to preach the gospel to the poor; he hath sent me to heal the brokenhearted, to preach deliverance to the captives, and recovering of sight to the blind, to set at liberty them that are bruised. Luke 4:18 KJV

 PRAYER

Dear God,

As I review everything that has happened in my life, I

THOUGHT 25: FINALLY

realize you have been there all along. Some choices I have made were a reaction to what happened to me. I was protecting myself from things I had no control over. I ask You for strength and courage today to do what I should have done a long time ago. Since I'm being totally honest, it has been hard to forgive people for what they did. It affected my decisions and relationships in my life. I can clearly see it formed my mind and emotions into something other than what You had intended for me. Now, it's time to move forward, not because I feel it, but because I understand that I cannot fully heal until I make the decision to forgive them. This is a starting point. God, help my heart to forgive so I can be whole again. I know it is a process so I ask You to heal my emotions so I can see things from Your point of view. I'm not waiting until I feel like it, I'm just choosing to forgive them.

My heart is learning to process the emotions, especially grief. I admit it is complicated, but not impossible. Help me to heal each time loss comes in my life. I understand that it is critical to give myself a lot of time to walk through all of the moments that will show up. I can't predict when they will come, I just know they will. I want to grow from these experiences as You teach me how to fully trust you with everything in my life. I know my head is in a better place of understanding and my broken heart is healing. Thank You for helping me to begin a new journey of wellness and wholeness. Amen.

MY HEAD KNOWS IT

CONCLUSION

There comes a time when we must make a truthful evaluation of ourselves. Grief takes us through a journey of self-examination. Some things that shift deep inside of us, only we know about. It is strange how loss changes many things about us. It can affect our level of anger, cause mistrust and increase impatience with challenging people. It can change our positive outlook to one of hopelessness and we may display the inability to complete tasks that were once simple to get done in a timely manner. We may become champions of causes, working ourselves to the point of exhaustion. Our passion may intensify in the short-term, but we may not be able to maintain the frantic pace of our fleeting ideas. The side effects of unresolved grief are many and diverse.

This season of loss can be a prime time for negative things to take a grip over our mind and heart. We could develop the attitude of "What's the use of even trying?" If we give in to toxic thinking the life we live after loss can become a dismal state of constant depression and darkness. To the dark person, everything has a dark perspective. We will find ourselves constantly looking for what is negative instead of seeing what is good. We will become void of any joy and soon people will move away from our space because they don't want to be around a constantly negative person.

On the other hand, we can use this time to really examine the lessons we should take away from our time of loss. What areas were exposed that we never recognized before? What tools did we discover that helped us improve ourselves? What are our new resolutions about living the rest of our life and sharing with others? How can we use what we have learned to help not only ourselves, but others?

Recently, I have had the opportunity for intense grief to visit me once again. My dear mother very recently has passed away. It truly feels confusing, knowing she wanted to be free from her pain and make her final journey to heaven yet, I needed her to stay here with us. Hmm, did I say needed? More accurately I should say, I wanted her to stay here. Our human side can be very selfish. It is hard to admit, but it is the truth. Though she suffered every day emotionally and physically, I still wanted her to be here with me! Releasing her was a necessary, voluntary act of my will not emotions. I didn't feel like letting her go. I knew I had to for her and for my personal well-being. As I spent the last moments with her, it all felt familiar. Memories flooded back from my father's passing. I resisted the inner voice of panic and placed my rushing emotions and hurting heart into God's hands. I prayed for peace when I wanted to run away and not face this again. I heard God's gentle voice whisper to my soul, "Trust me. It is well with her soul. It's time to let her go." As my two siblings and I embraced the last moments, we each had our time to tell her we loved her. The gentle touches of reassurance and comfort eased the transition. These seemingly small gestures close doors that shouldn't be left open. Everyone may not have these types of opportunities due to varied circumstances, but we all must find a way to complete the life cycle. Releasing them to death is a vital piece to the puzzle of life. Releasing them will be an ongoing process not a one-time occurrence. The reality will begin to set in as we find ways to move forward. This is acceptance, full circle.

I celebrate her and grieve the loss of her at the same time! The celebration is not an outward party or display of joy, rather it's more of a resolve that this is the end of her earthly journey. Her reward is waiting for her. I really can't imagine what heaven must be like. I just know it is wonderful.

Now we see things imperfectly, like puzzling reflections in a mirror, but then we will see everything with perfect clarity. All that I know now is partial and incomplete, but then I will know everything completely, just as God now knows me completely.
1 Corinthians 13:12 NLT

My heart rejoices knowing she is seeing those she has missed so much on this side, but most of all seeing Jesus in peace! All of her questions are answered and most of all she has found the peace she was missing. There is no more pain, suffering or grief, only joy. My mom is now complete in Christ and in her new home, heaven. Though my head can process this information the waves of pain in my heart still come. There are so many moments of spontaneous tears when memories of her flood my mind, understanding they are all I have left. I must say it feels a lot different when both of your parents are gone. I must now navigate life with the principles my parents have instilled in me. I am forced to trust this process. It feels like the training wheels of life have just been taken off my bicycle. I've been in training all along, now it is time to do it truly on my own.

There is a bit of an "orphan syndrome," even though I am an adult. There is something very foundational and grounding when our parents are still with us. Once they are gone, we no longer have access to phone calls or conversations about anything. The void that is left can be deafening. We may find ourselves picking up the phone to dial them only to realize, we can't. I've seen people keep voice messages long after they have passed. Once again, this is normal. We all cope differently with personal loss. Hearing their voice may be a comfort and reassurance that they are not forgotten even though they are gone. Keep this in a healthy perspective, however. Do not become so obsessed with the past that you can't move forward to living in the present. In time, we will learn to celebrate their lives without the tears. Comfort may be slow to arrive. With the passage of time, it will slowly manifest with acceptance of what you cannot change.

There may be more questions about your personal loss than answers, but that is what discovery is about. The survivor's guilt we may feel after someone is gone can keep us from making progress towards healing. Often, we focus on what we didn't do while they were alive rather than deciding to do better going forward. There is nothing we can do to change history. We can control what we decide to do now. That means we must take responsibility for our own recovery from loss.

Keep asking God probing questions. He's not intimidated by our curiosity. It builds a great relationship when we are honest with what we feel. Continue to practice healing techniques, praying, reading, journaling, meditation, talking to God and others, join support groups, the list goes on. Do what works best for you.

I am sorry that loss arrived in your life. I do hope that in some way, this book is the horizon of a new, informed life for you. You will always carry the scar of your loss, but God can heal the pain underneath your scar so you can bear it. It will become a reminder of just how far you have come.

My head knows just how hard this journey is. Grief and loss are a part of it, but now my heart can understand that God has brought me this far and will continue to walk with me for the rest of my life. The path is not smooth, clear, or simple. No one lives forever. I understand grief will come again and I must process it each time it occurs. Hopefully, we will all be a little better equipped to walk through it when it arrives. Please remember, just keep moving forward. At first, it may feel as if we are not making any progress at all. Each new journey begins by placing one foot in front of the other, even when we don't feel like it. That's when we walk by faith not by what we see right now. When we look back as time passes, we will be able to see how far we have really come. No one chooses this path. Grief chooses us, every one of us.

As once again I walk through new territory I don't feel quite as alone. My heart still hurts, but I know the sun will shine again. I'm going to be alright, in time. This time, I will give myself permission to be human, to cry, to grieve, to feel all of it including the joy and the pain. God has never left me. He's right here, just like always.

PRAYER

Dear God,

Here we are again, same story, different day. Sometimes being human is extremely painful. I'm really trying to take each day as it comes to me. You will give me what I need to get through today. I'm going to let tomorrow take care of itself. I'm asking again for help with the emotions that come from nowhere! Give me the strength to make it through this. The tears are real and so is my pain. I know I can do this if I allow You to help me. Heal me when it's time. In the meantime, I'm giving You my fragile heart to keep while I grieve. Thank You for being such a faithful God when it's good and when it's hard. I am so glad You are helping me adjust my mind during this season. I'm finding peace even in the middle of my storm because You are in the center of the storm with me. As I learn to lean on You, I am finding comfort. Thank You for helping us all to navigate our way through our pain of loss. You want us to be whole again. My Head knows it, now my heart...can understand. Amen.

www.ingramcontent.com/pod-product-compliance
Lightning Source LLC
Chambersburg PA
CBHW072015110526
44592CB00012B/1314